A Different Side of Hollywood:
White Girls Don't Get Shot

By Amanda L. Updegraff

PublishAmerica
Baltimore

© 2006 by Amanda L. Updegraff.
All rights reserved. No part of this book may be reproduced, stored in a retrieval system or transmitted in any form or by any means without the prior written permission of the publishers, except by a reviewer who may quote brief passages in a review to be printed in a newspaper, magazine or journal.

First printing

At the specific preference of the author, PublishAmerica allowed this work to remain exactly as the author intended, verbatim, without editorial input.

ISBN: 1-4241-0980-9
PUBLISHED BY PUBLISHAMERICA, LLLP
www.publishamerica.com
Baltimore

Printed in the United States of America

Scripture taken from the HOLY BIBLE, NEW INTERNATIONAL VERSION. Copyright 1973, 1978, 1984 by International Bible Society. Used by permission of Zondervan Publishing House. All rights reserved.

Dedication

For my parents, Jim and Penny,
who have faithfully loved each other and me

Acknowledgments

First, I must thank my family. My parents have supported, encouraged, and loved me unconditionally. They have been one of the greatest blessings that God has given to me. To my brother, Derek, you are the true writer and poet of the family. I am so happy for your friendship. Thank you for your editorial help and creative suggestions. Elizabeth, you are the sister I have always wanted. Our family has been enriched by your presence. I am grateful to the Indiana Updegraff's, Ann, Randy, Andrew and Claire, for being my home and my refuge throughout college. Thank you also to the New York/Arizona Updegraff's and the Swackhamer clan. My grandma Swack and my granddad Updegraff were wonderful people who are dearly missed.

I am indebted to everyone who has been a part of the Hollywood Urban Project and the neighbors in my community. I have been humbled, challenged, and transformed by my experience with HUP. Many thanks to the board members, citydweller alumni, donors, staff, volunteers, and Nancy Walker Litteken who followed the call to be a bridge between the church and the community.

My friends have been one of the greatest joys of my life, and I cannot express with words what it has meant to have companions such as these: The D-4 girls (Mariah Sirkin, Molly Shoup and Gina Stebing), Amy Webster, and Anissa Steinborn. This book would not have happened if it weren't for the stories of my HUP friends and community. I am grateful to Nancy Hunter, Christine Showler, Rob Jackson, Carrie Boren and Stacey Porter for being my partners on this journey. Carey Smith, DeJuan Ruffin, Kari McFarland, Amy Gatje Santamaria, Cindy Guerten, Catherine and Alastair Rundle, and all of the members of the extended community have been my kindred spirits. Thank you also to Autumn Fiore, Diana Salazar, Cynthia Zatkin, Rebecca Snavely, and Annette Lopez for your faithful friendship.

I have also been blessed with a wonderful church family: Tribe of Los Angeles (www.tribela.com). Reverand Rebecca, your support and encouragement in this project means so much to me. I am thankful to be a part of such a creative, unique, and faithful group of people. Many thanks to my friend, Kevin Rolly, the talented photographer who shot the front cover and author photos (www.kevissimo.com).

Thank you also to the following people: Scott Porter, my lawyer, and Dale and Kathy Bruner for giving me the courage to pursue publication. I am very grateful to Michael Evans for his work in editing this book and improving it greatly.

Table of Contents

Chapter 1
Stardom
11

Chapter 2
Road Trip
19

Chapter 3
Hollywood
25

Chapter 4
Mexico
37

Chapter 5
English as a Second Language
43

Chapter 6
Neighborhood Youth
53

Chapter 7
Animal Planet
61

Chapter 8
Apartment #5
69

Chapter 9
Charlie's Angel
81

Chapter 10
The Unicorn
83

Chapter 11
Depression
93

Chapter 12
Alberto
109

Chapter 13
The Dangerous Blonde
125

Chapter 14
A Birthday Celebration
129

Chapter 15
Juan
139

Chapter 16
African-American Spirituality
147

Chapter 17
Community
155

Chapter 18
Rekindled Hope
161

Stardom

In May of 1998, I set out for Hollywood to find my own kind of fame. I loaded four suitcases and my newly acquired diploma from the University of Indianapolis into the 1986 Buick Regal that I had inherited from my granddad. The Regal was a huge, white beast complete with a felt ceiling that was caving in, a large dent on the back left hand side, and pipe holders on the dashboard. It looked like a car that would be owned by an elderly person or a gang member. My granddad had smoked a pipe until about ten years before his death, but he had never removed the two metal pipe holders. When I got the car, there was a half eaten pack of lifesaver mints in one of the holders. My granddad was well known for his mint stash. Everyone in our family is very sentimental about the bright blue pack of lifesavers that peers out at us from its place in the grocery store line.

Of course all of my college friends had wanted rides in my flashy new car and I was happy to oblige. We could pile three people in the front seat and up to four in the back. It never failed that someone would reach into the pipe holder and grab the half eaten pack of lifesavers. I would screech the car to a halt, reach across and tear the precious roll from the hands of a stunned friend.

"Those mints belonged to my granddad and he is dead. They are not to be eaten," I would say as my friends stared at me in disbelief.

Finally, I ended up eating all of the mints because this scenario happened just about every time someone new got in my car. I put all of the mints in my mouth at once, about eight of them, closed my eyes, and remembered trying to choose which hand my granddad had hidden them in when I was a little girl. The hand I had picked would open up to reveal a shiny dime sitting on his palm. I would pout and say, "Granddaddy," in a whiny tone. He would put his hands behind his back and I would try again. This time, a perfectly round, white mint with a hole in the middle was the prize.

I only saw my grandfather about once a year as I was growing up because he lived in Florida and my family settled in San Diego. He moved to Indianapolis in order to be near his daughter, my aunt Ann, at the same time I moved there to attend the University of Indianapolis. I saw him almost once a week in the two years before he passed away.

My granddad had digestive problems and would randomly burp extremely loud. My six-year-old cousin, Andrew, found this hysterical. He couldn't quite understand why it was all right for granddaddy to burp like that but he got in trouble when he let one roar.

At the beginning of my junior year of college, my grandfather was hospitalized. Ann called me with the news and I borrowed a friend's car and drove immediately over to their house. My uncle, Randy, and I went to the hospital together. My granddad looked like a child swaddled in the hospital blankets. I leaned down and hugged him, feeling like a child myself as I whispered, "Hi Granddaddy." Randy spoke to Granddad as if everything was normal, asking him how he was feeling and telling him about what was happening outside of the hospital walls. I felt like I was watching it all from a distance, invisible to my family and passing nurses. Before it was time to go, Randy suggested we pray. I became visible and entered into the huddle around the bed, holding Granddad's hand on one side and Randy's on the other. Randy prayed for healing and comfort and strength for our family. Tears began to roll down my face as I entertained the possibility that my granddad might die. I gently pulled my hand out of his grasp and wiped the tears away. When I placed my wet hand back in his, I wondered how much longer I could hold on to him. I made sure to memorize the roughness of his palms and the peaks and valleys of wrinkles and veins. I marveled that this was the same hand that hid mints from me so many years ago.

That night I lay in bed and thought about how little I really knew about my grandfather. I had lived near him for two years and hadn't taken the opportunity to find out about his life or what my father had been like as a boy. I never asked him to tell me stories about my grandma, who died before I was born. Those two years had been all about me. My main concern had been to have fun and party with my friends, not hang out with an old man.

When my granddad passed away, I mourned not only his death, but also the time that I had missed when he was alive.

The Buick was my reminder, not just a way to get from here to there. The junky car with its thumbtacked felt ceiling, rusty edges and vinyl roof kept telling me to pay attention and listen to the stories of my passengers. I began to write letters to my one remaining grandparent, my mother's mom. I would tell her that she was in my thoughts and that school was going well, omitting the details about my life outside of the classroom. My grandma would write back and tell me that she loved me and was proud of me, which made me feel wonderful and guilty at the same time. I felt that if she knew the way I had really been living, my grandma would have been disappointed rather than proud.

It didn't take long for me to go back to my selfish and self-absorbed ways after my brief encounter with conviction. My granddad had died at the beginning of my junior year and by Christmas time, I was back to living a self-indulgent life. I drank rum and coke religiously and went out clubbing every week from Wednesday through Saturday. I danced on the countertops of bars, thriving on attention from men and jealous looks from women.

I hadn't always been like this. I grew up as a Christian, which meant that I went to church, never drank, and didn't even think about having sex until I was married. My parents took me to church for the first time when I was three days old. Ever since I can remember knowing anything, I knew about God. My Mom would tuck me into bed at night and say, "Mama loves you and Jesus loves you."

When I was five years old, I had one of the most profound spiritual experiences of my life. I remember sitting at the side of my house with my back pressed against the stucco and my bare feet digging into the mud. I closed my eyes and prayed out loud with all of the intensity and fervor that I could muster in my little body that God's kingdom would come. In my mind, I envisioned the fight between God and Satan, and I wanted God to win. There was not an ounce of doubt about God's goodness and power that could distract me from praying. Over and over I asked God to beat Satan so that the world would know what I knew about God. I prayed so passionately that tears fell freely down my face. The sun set and I sat in darkness, unwilling to end my plea to God.

As the years went by, I continued to go to Sunday school and learn about Jesus and Bible stories. I believed that Jesus was God's son who died on the cross. I didn't think much about the implications of this or why it mattered outside of having to spend my Sunday mornings at church. As I got older, particularly in junior high, church and God became less interesting to me. My mom forced me and my brother to get out of bed on Sundays and go to church. She tried for three years to convince me to attend the youth group. Finally, during my sophomore year, I agreed to go on a trip the youth group was taking to the mountains. On that trip, I discovered an incentive to attend church one extra day per week. It turned out that there were cute guys at youth group.

Gradually, I could feel myself changing on the inside. Faith in God became more than something I saw in my parents. They set an example for me of what it meant to follow Christ, and now this faith was becoming my own. The Jesus who I had always believed in was becoming more than just a guy up in heaven, watching from afar. I began to desire to know Him and talk to Him. I wanted to follow His teachings and lead my life in a way that would be pleasing to Him. Some people have an experience where they come to know God in an epiphany of thunder and lightning. My experience was more like an extended period of noticing little light bulbs coming on one at a time to illuminate my path.

Now, I have a deep respect and gratitude to my parents, especially my mom, for her fervent prayers and deep desire for me to know God. When you discover something so amazing and life changing, you want to share it with the people you love. My mom trusted and waited patiently for both of her children to enter into that fullness of life.

My faith in God was genuine, but I became very legalistic. I created a list for myself that I stored in my head of all the things that I was supposed to be doing and all of the things that I absolutely could not do. I followed that list intently, refusing to compromise. My faith often turned into an outside show of morality rather than an inner communion with God. I was a committed Christian by my junior year of high school, and I attended Bible studies rather than parties. This continued through my freshman year of college.

At the end of my freshman year, I did something that I never dreamed I would do. I succumbed to peer pressure and got drunk at the house of some of the senior girls on my basketball team. They were all drinking margaritas, and for the first time, my desire to fit in overtook the checklist that I had followed so closely. I never intended to get drunk, however. I was handed a glass that was full to the brim with a strawberry margarita and I cautiously took it in my hands, as if it contained lighter fluid. My intention was only to have a few sips of the evil alcoholic beverage. I put the glass tenderly to my lips and barely wet my tongue with the first sip. When lightning didn't come down from the sky to strike me dead, I took another sip. I had always treated alcohol like poison, so it startled me to discover that the margarita was actually delicious. While the rest of the girls talked and flirted with the guys who had stopped by, I sat quietly on the couch and sipped that margarita until it was gone. I stood up to walk home as the party was dispersing, and a wave of nausea hit me and forced me back onto the couch. Suddenly, I felt hot all over, and my head was spinning. Finally, I made it off the couch, carefully put one foot in front of the other, and began the walk across campus to my dorm. The whole way I kept repeating to myself, "I am drunk, I am drunk," over and over in my head because it just didn't seem possible. The next day, I vomited three times in the morning and my roommate felt so sorry for me because I told her I had the flu. I wasn't about to let my nasty little secret out in the open for people to see that my goody two shoes record had been tarnished.

Besides the unpleasantness of heaving in the communal dorm room bathroom, I discovered something that shocked me: drinking wasn't that big of a deal. Nobody died. Jesus didn't come down and drag me to hell. I got a little sick, but the day went on as normal, just as all the others had before. Even so, I resigned not to do it again because Christians don't do that sort of thing.

I went home to San Diego for the summer and repented. I came back to Indianapolis for my sophomore year and ended up at a party during the first week of school. Those parties with alcohol and people acting wild had always seemed like a ridiculous waste of time to me. I don't know what led me to change my views, let go of my rigidity and join in on the fun. Maybe I was seeking attention or testing God. Maybe I was sick of the rules and of trying to be perfect.

This began a spiritual crisis in my life that lasted about two and a half years, minus a brief reprieve after my granddad's death. I felt that I couldn't claim to be a Christian while experimenting with the things that I had shunned. But my curiosity was piqued and I wanted to explore all of the things that my list forbade me to do. I told God that I was taking a hiatus from my faith. I still believed in Him and in the truth of His word, but I wanted to sow my wild oats and found my Christian life boring compared to what others around me were doing. I knew that I would come back to my faith one day and that I wasn't abandoning it forever. I actually told God that when I was old, maybe when I turned forty, I would become a Christian again.

And so it began. There were parties and clubs and alcohol and men. For the next two years, I put aside the faith and convictions that had been so important and tried to replace the vacancy they left with other things. The hole left by the absence of my relationship with God started out small and began to get deeper. The more I tried to fill it with partying and men, the wider the hole became. But I was stubborn and unwilling to accept that maybe I had made a mistake.

As I began my senior year of college, my brother, Derek, left home after graduating from high school to do a yearlong program called Mission Year. He moved to Oakland with a team of four other people, serving a local church, working at the county jail, and ministering to inmates on death row. He sent monthly letters to his supporters about his ministry and the way his life was being changed. Derek's letters affected me deeply, and reminded me what it was like to live in light of God's love. I longed for God to fill the emptiness that I had created within myself, but I didn't know how to get back to that place. Saying sorry and abandoning the way I had been living didn't seem like enough. I had forgotten how to pray and just be with God.

My journey back to faith was a lot like the way it began. I spent several months noticing light bulbs coming on here and there to light the way back to God. The hole in my heart was slowly closing and I began to feel more peace than I had in a long time.

As I began to think about what I would do after graduation, I was inspired by Derek to do a year of service. I wanted the same type of life changing experience that he had written about and I was eager to live as a reflection of my faith. I contacted my high school youth pastor and he gave me information on the various young adult mission sites of the Presbyterian Church, U.S.A. I wasn't quite ready to go to Africa or India, so I looked up the descriptions of the domestic mission organizations. I was immediately drawn to the Hollywood Urban Project (HUP), which had a one-year internship in urban ministry called City Dwellers. The neighborhood HUP served was inhabited almost entirely by Latino immigrants and the focus of HUP was to build relationships with neighbors, and be a light in the community. This was perfect because it was close to my home in San

Diego and I speak Spanish. I filled out the application and had an interview with the director, Dan Hoffman, at the yearly discernment convention for potential Presbyterian missionaries. It became clear that Hollywood was calling me.

Most people move to Hollywood with high hopes of fame and fortune, a suitcase full of trendy clothes and idealistic fantasies of seeing their name in lights. My dream was to save the world, starting with the sixteen blocks between Vine Street and Gower, Santa Monica Boulevard and Melrose. On the surface, it seemed sacrificial and honorable, but vanity was hidden deep within me. Mixed in with the genuine hope of making a difference and serving others was the desire for people to think I was particularly special and spiritual for being a missionary. I could not fully let go of the desire to be admired, and I sought it in the holy as much as I had in the profane. The Catholic priest, Henri Nouwen, has struggled with the same need to be noticed. In his book, *The Genesee Diary*, Nouwen describes his own inner battle. He wanted to do something different or special that would result in stardom. The need to be set apart was part of the driving force behind his lifestyle.

In the same way that Nouwen secretly desires stardom, I too set out for Hollywood to become some sort of star.

Road Trip

My good friend, Amy, was very brave and agreed to drive the Buick with me from Indianapolis to San Diego. We watched the movie, *Thelma and Louise*, before we left and had big dreams of adventure on the open road.

The day before our scheduled departure, I was frantically going through my belongings, shoving some things in suitcases while trying to pawn others off onto my friends. My poor roommates ended up with the ceramic chicken, a six foot by ten foot Abercrombie and Fitch poster of guys in their boxers, and some other odds and ends. As I was going through my clothes, I weeded out all of the hoochie items that I used to wear to clubs and parties. These included any shirts that showed my stomach or cleavage and my favorite black pants that were way too tight. Throwing those clothes into the Goodwill bag was symbolic of the new way of life I had chosen. I was on my way to do God's work and I didn't think He appreciated those clothes.

Amy and I tearfully said goodbye to my roommates who had

become like sisters to me and drove away from Indianapolis, heading toward my grandma's house in Missouri. With every second that passed, I was getting further and further away from the best friends I had ever had, a man who I thought I might marry someday, and my extended family that showered me with love and support. For those first few hours, I felt nothing but sadness. Amy and I drove in silence as I wondered what this journey would mean for those friendships that were so dear.

It was a clear ending to a tumultuous relationship with a man who did not beg me to stay. He let me go and I would have gone even if he had put up a fight. I thought that he should have shown up with an orchestra serenading me and written "Don't Go" in rose petals on my street. I wanted a dramatic movie ending with a passionate plea and tears. I inched the Buick down my street, thinking that he might show up at the last minute, jump in front of my car and tell me that he couldn't possibly imagine his life without me. But he didn't show up, and now I was leaving him behind along with the ceramic chicken and scantily clad Abercrombie models. It was an anticlimactic finale to a rollercoaster relationship.

All that I was leaving behind meant that there was something new to be found. I was going on an adventure to find my true calling, my destiny and myself. It seemed so romantic and novel. Somewhere at the edge of the Indiana state border, I stopped looking behind and began to enjoy the journey. Amy and I talked and tried to find a radio station that played something other than country music and talked some more. We got excited about huge truck stops and cattle grazing. We felt free, heading toward California without a time frame or fixed agenda.

The first stop on our tour was my grandma's house in St. Joseph, Missouri. I was excited that Amy would get a chance to meet my grandma and my aunt, Jeanette. They are such kind and gentle women and the essence of what it means to be Godly. Jeanette has taken countless people under her wing and cared for them. In the presence of these women, I know that I have the potential to be more fully alive in my relationship with God than I am, and they inspire me to seek Him much more than I do.

My grandma's house contains pictures on every wall and tabletop of her children, grandchildren, and great-grandchildren. She will never forget what I look like. One of my favorite pictures is a portrait of my mom when she was in the eighth grade. She had perfect, wavy blonde hair and a pretty smile. When I was younger, I used to look at that picture and hope that I would look like her one day. I have always known that my mom is beautiful and feared that I am not.

The day after we arrived, Amy and I took my grandma to an iris garden that she had wanted to see. I expected to find a patch of land with some flowers here and there, but the garden was actually fields of irises that stretched as far as I could see. I took my grandma's hand and helped her walk through the rows of flowers. She was getting unsteadier on her feet and couldn't walk as easily as she used to. We went slowly along as my grandma bent down to examine the color and texture of each individual iris, as if it were one of God's unique children. Her body had become frail and delicate, yet she possessed a visible strength that could not be trampled by age. My grandma looked at home in the open field and a bit naked without a hoe and some gloves. I half expected her to kneel down and begin digging in the dirt. Whenever I had thoughts of my grandma, I envisioned her working in the garden, planting vegetables, and pointing my aunts in the direction of a bush that needed to be removed. Some families gather around the television. We gathered around the yard, pulling weeds, trimming hedges, and gathering asparagus.

After a while, Amy and I ran ahead and explored the field. We were delighted with the flowers as well, and marveled at the beauty of creation. I looked up to check on my grandma and saw her about fifty feet away. She stood with her back slightly hunched forward, slowly turning around in circles and looking about. My grandma looked like a lost child, and I realized that she was looking for me. I shouted, "I'm over here, Grandma," but she didn't hear me. She kept looking around for a sign of someone she knew. I began to run through the row of flowers and jumped over irises to get to her. I came up beside her and put my arm around her shoulder, whispering in her ear that she was okay and I was right there with her. Holding my grandma, I got a glimpse of what it felt like to be a mother. It was a rush of warmth and tenderness with a twinge of anxiety. There was such beauty in the enormity of responsibility, of being needed, depended upon.

Amy and I left Missouri after two days and began to make our way through Kansas and Nebraska. That was the last time I saw my grandma before she was confined to a wheelchair. I am so grateful for the memory of standing with her among the irises.

Somewhere, in the middle of Texas, the novelty of a road trip wore off. We drove for hours on a highway surrounded by dirt. Amy managed to find a Texas highway patrol man who pulled her over for speeding. She escaped with a warning and wasn't given a ticket because she looks like Kim Basinger and I could see that he was smitten.

A few hours later, we came across a sign that said, "State prison ahead—Do not pick up hitchhikers." We pulled over in front of the sign and took turns taking each other's picture. We stood for a few minutes with our thumbs sticking up, hoping that someone would drive by and find us amusing, but we were out in the middle of nowhere all alone.

The next item of interest we passed was the largest cross in the United States. Of course it is in Texas. We drove by, acknowledged that the cross was indeed very large, and prayed that we would be out of Texas soon. Our next major stop was the Grand Canyon, and we longed to be out of the car and surrounded by beauty.

Like idiots, Amy and I hiked four miles into the Grand Canyon without sunscreen or water bottles. At the end point of the hike, we found a place to lie down, and looked up only to realize that the hike back up would be even more exhausting. Neither of us had the strength to drag our baked skin, dry mouths, nor aching feet back to the top. The only thing that gave me the ability to hike back up was the hope of a water fountain. I fantasized and maybe even hallucinated about the feel of cool water running down my throat.

Amy and I decided that our last destination before reaching San

Diego should be Las Vegas. "Vegas, baby, Vegas." I quoted the movie, *Swingers*, as we made our way past the Hoover Dam toward the beckoning lights of the city. Amy had a friend who lived there and he invited us to stay in his apartment. Once we arrived at his place, we cleaned up and sat in front of the mirror, fixing our hair and make-up as we had done many nights before in preparation to go dancing. I opened my suitcase and discovered that my black pants had jumped out of the Goodwill bag and into my suitcase. I lay across the bed and forced them over my hips, sucking in my stomach as I pulled up the zipper.

Amy's friend, Sam, was eager to show off the city. He paraded us through all of the nice hotels and we ended up at Studio 54, a dance club inside the MGM Grand. My black pants felt at home and made their way to the dance floor. It was a new city but a familiar scene, as I had to surround Amy and protect her from swarming men. Men who didn't even bother to ask if she would like to dance often attacked her from all sides. Minus a few interruptions, we danced until the early morning. I spent the evening drinking coke, without the rum, and felt that I behaved myself in a nice, Christian manner.

The next day, we slept until two o'clock in the afternoon. Amy and I gathered our belongings, thanked our wonderful host, and began the drive to our final destination. Six hours later, the Buick brought us safely to the warmth and familiarity of my parent's house in San Diego.

I had the rest of the summer to prepare for my next adventure, a one-year stint in Hollywood.

Hollywood

In September of 1998, I loaded my belongings back into the Buick and made the two-hour drive up to Hollywood. There were seven other people who had been selected to be city dwellers, and they were to be my new roommates. We moved into two connected apartments (one for men and one for women), each with two bedrooms and one bathroom. It was like the MTV reality show, *The Real World*, minus the cameras, hot tub, posh house, and romantic hook ups. There were four men: Abel from Alaska, Bobby from South Carolina, Scott from California, and Neil from England. There were also three other women: Christine from California, Dyhanne from England, and Fritze from North Carolina. We were all thrown together, and the most we had in common was that none of us knew what we had gotten ourselves into for the next year of our lives.

I had a more difficult time getting along with Abel than any of the other seven. He was a native Alaskan and looked every bit the part, from his long wavy hair, to the distinct features of his nostrils and jawbone. Abel was just a boy at nineteen. He was financially irresponsible and could not wake up on time, which pushed all of my buttons. Abel was a carnivore in the purest sense, like a lion or a bear. He talked incessantly about meat, and could eat all of us under the table. Abel also loved the rain. While the rest of us remained inside during a storm, clothed in sweaters and wool socks, Abel would stand outside on the porch wearing a t-shirt and shorts, his feet uncovered. I would look out the window and see him soaked to the bone with his eyes closed, dreaming that he was on a fishing boat and catching salmon.

Bobby was a nerd in the best possible way. Halfway through seminary, he decided to take a year off from school. Bobby was incredibly book smart and started many intense theological debates in the men's apartment. He had red hair with a little cowlick in the middle of his forehead, and freckles on his cheeks. He had a good sense of humor, revealing a twinge of silliness despite being rather serious. His laugh was like that of a child, a mischievous sort of giggle. One of my favorite accomplishments was to make Bobby laugh.

Scott came to us from the mountains and never quite felt right in the city. His six foot five inch frame might have appeared intimidating, but Scott was a gentle giant. He arrived in Hollywood driving a super cool, orange jeep. As soon as I saw it, I knew that I needed to explore the city in that fine vehicle. Sadly, it died shortly after its debut in L.A., and the jeep became nothing more than a lawn ornament. I sort of became Scott's sidekick. Much of our free time was spent together, and I always felt like he understood me.

Neil was the goofball of the group and we had many good laughs at his expense. We all watched him eagerly as our group made a new acquaintance, because nobody could ever understand him when he said his name. He would say, "Hi, I'm Neil," in his English accent, and the stranger would squint their eyes, tilt their head, and in a confused tone, repeat, "Nail?"

"No, Nee-yul," he would say again, doing his best American accent. When I first met Neil, I had never seen anyone so pale, and I stared at his white skin in disbelief. He had a distinct, European look, with dark shorts and sandals. Neil serenaded us with his guitar playing and singing, which caused a few tiffs in the guy's apartment. Sometimes, he acted like a baby to get his way, and we would all throw in the towel when the whining started.

    Christine was the most agreeable and easy going of the group. She would go along with anything, which left only seven of us to argue over what to eat for dinner. Christine was kind and gentle, a good listener and a good friend. All of the men in the singles group at church had their eyes on her. Christine's one fault was that she was the tiniest bit messy. She and I shared a room, and it was a rare moment when the carpet could be seen. Our bedroom had a loft, and Christine had to climb a ladder to get to her bed. Sometimes, I would climb up with her and we would imagine what it would be like to jump off, miss the ceiling fan, and land on my bed.

    I loved Dyhanne from the moment I met her. She said things like "lovely" and "You're mad" in her English accent. Dhyanne called me babe and the sound of her voice was sweet and soothing. Unlike her British counterpart, Neil, she had great style. I thought she was stunning and so did the men who whistled at her as she waited for the bus. The two of us clicked and Dhyanne became like a sister to me. She often got mistaken for Lauren Hill as we shopped on Melrose. The thrill of a new purchase was something we both appreciated when we could afford it.

    Fritze had beautiful, olive skin and perfectly straight hair that always looked good. She wore Birkenstocks and never put on a bit of make-up. There was something about Fritze that made her seem elusive and mysterious. I couldn't quite capture who she was. The little girls in the neighborhood adored her, and must have known the secret. Fritze got engaged over our Thanksgiving vacation to a man who fell in love with her when she showed him a dance that she had made up to the song, "Turning Japanese."

Our neighborhood consisted of sixteen blocks and housed thousands of people. The tour buses and producers in their BMW convertibles had to pass through the tagged up buildings and run down apartments to get to Paramount studios. Rounding the corner on Gower Street and heading past Paramount around 8:00 a.m., I came across a neatly formed line of middle aged, white women wearing business suits, eager for some helpful advice from Dr. Phil.

Besides for my teammates and other former city dwellers who had stayed in the neighborhood after their year of service, the neighborhood was mostly inhabited by Latino immigrants from Mexico, Guatemala, and El Salvador. Many of the adults did not speak English, though most of the children did. The Hollywood Urban Project owned a house on Gregory Street that was called the community house. The living room was the site for English as a second language classes, an after school program, Young Life (a Christian youth group), and various meetings. The house had two bedrooms, which were used as an office and a computer/tutoring room. The living room was in the front of the house and the two bedrooms were off to the side. The walls of each room were painted with bright colors, canary yellow, and peptobismol pink. The carpet was a lost cause. I think at one time it must have been blue, but when I arrived it was a sad mixture of dirt and stains. Straight on through the living room were the kitchen and a small laundry area. The backyard was a blacktop with a basketball hoop and space for a few cars. In back of the house, on the left side, were the city dweller apartments, where my teammates and I lived. The apartments were built by Habitat for Humanity, as well as by faithful members of the First Presbyterian Church of Hollywood and other HUP supporters.

Those first few weeks of living in Hollywood were interesting, to say the least. My teammates and I were trying to get to know each other, learn our roles in this ministry, and get used to a new surrounding. Dan, our director, had us take prayer walks around the neighborhood to become more familiar with the area and get a sense of both the needs and the joys. Among the things that caught my eye were the graffiti, or tagging as I later learned it was called, adorning many of the buildings, as well as the lack of open space and vegetation. Buildings seemed to be piled on top of buildings. There was no place other than the street for children to play.

The striking difference between my suburban life and this urban jungle was even more pronounced in the sounds than in the sights. I had never paid attention to the role of sound in my daily life, probably because noise in the suburbs is not an issue. I didn't notice sound because there wasn't any. But in my new home, my ears were constantly ringing with some new tune. First of all, there were the different types of noises for the various venders. The fruit truck that sold, well, fruit, as well as bread, eggs, milk, and toys, played the song *La Cucaracha* as it announced its arrival onto our street. The ice cream truck chimed in with *It's a Small World*. Then there were the individual entrepreneurs, who took their home baked goods to the streets. One lady pushed her baby tamales in a stroller and honked a hand held horn. Another lady carried her goods in grocery sacks hanging from both arms and shouted, "E-L-O-T-E-S." Combined with the noises of selling were the screams of children as they came home from school and ran into the community house. And let's not forget the music from home stereo systems and parked cars with all of the doors open and not a soul in the driver's seat. Here, we had our choice of rap music or ranchero/mariachi. Car alarms and police helicopters overhead rounded out the symphony.

Another thing I noticed as I explored Hollywood was the extraordinary amount of attractive people in one town. All of the gorgeous people from all over the world who have ever been told that they should be actors or models, had come to Hollywood to try their luck. And so, the most beautiful people congregated in this one little town to make everyone else feel ordinary. All of the insecurities that rage inside me about my body and physical appearance began working overtime.

In the midst of this world of incredibly handsome people, I found one place of comfort. This place of refuge was the women's locker room at the YMCA. Okay, there were still some of those models walking around with flawless skin and zero fat, but there was also a contingency of seniors who were devoted to water aerobics. They pranced around the locker room stark naked, before and after class, showing off each saggy breast and wrinkled butt cheek as if they had won them at the fair. I used to linger by my locker a little longer than was necessary because I was able to think to myself, "Damn, I look good."

In becoming acquainted with the neighborhood, Dan had some of the youth come and talk to us about gangs and tagging. There were three gangs in the neighborhood: The Magician's Club (T.M.C.), the Rebels, and 18th Street (who were part of the Mexican Mafia and stretch all through out Los Angeles). The two former gangs were smaller and limited to our neighborhood. The gangs left their marks on buildings, claiming their territory. Spray painting, or tagging, was done in the name of the gang or the individual member. The letters T.M.C. were a prominent feature on the side of apartment buildings, as well as the name a youth is given when they get jumped into a gang. The trouble would begin when someone would cross out a name and write his or her own.

In addition to gangs, there were other less harmful tagging crews or taggers. Some youth who were not necessarily involved in a gang would participate in the defamation of property through tagging. These kids were in danger of getting in deeper and joining gangs.

There were families in my neighborhood that had been gang banging for generations. I know some youth whose grandparents were gang members and they brought their children up in this lifestyle. Youth, particularly junior high boys, got jumped into gangs. The youth literally gets surrounded and beaten, sometimes with knives or bottles, and are forced to join the gang. The youth are not asked if they would like to participate. There is no choice unless they want the beatings to continue.

One teenager named Jeremy, who was active in the community house and participated in a Bible study for high school boys, was horribly attacked on his way home from school one day. He did not want to be in the gang, but he was terrified of what would happen if he refused. Jeremy did not leave his house to go to school or the community house. Finally, his family moved to South Central to get him away from the situation.

The neighborhood contains a lot of pain and brokenness, but the hope and love that I experienced there was above and beyond anything I even imagined existed. It was a great privilege to be surrounded by people who have overcome the challenges of poverty and oppression. My neighbors were poor when it came to finances, but they were abundantly wealthy in the areas of courage, family support, and love. The reason that so many people are crammed into a sixteen-block area is because families of four to ten people are living in studios, one and two bedroom apartments. Often, extended families of cousins, aunts and grandparents all live together in order to afford the rent. There is such a strong sense of family, of caring for one another and making sure that nobody is left out on the street. Family is cherished. Arms are open and extended to embrace even those who are not kin into the family.

Many of the barriers of prejudice that I had held about the poor were broken down daily. I had actually thought, in the back of my little mind, that they did not love their children as much, didn't have as much interest in education, and lacked moral backbone. These are things that I would never have admitted, and I am sure nobody would have thought I was the type of person who could harbor such horrible and ridiculous thoughts. Part of the prejudice was the tendency to believe that the way I was raised is the right way. I felt superior because of my white skin and education. Somehow, my opinion was more important, my life was more valuable, and my future was more promising. All of these judgments and feelings of ethnocentrism rose up within me as soon as I left the dominant white culture that I had been surrounded by my whole life. Living in a community where my way of doing things was not the norm showed me the depth of my pride.

One family in particular challenged all of my preconceived ideas and forced me to move beyond prejudice and racism into truth. The Ramirez family consisted of Julio, the father who worked as a carpenter, Norma, the mother who was a homemaker, and five children, Tito, Tomas, Rosa, Carolina, and Mari Elena. The seven of them lived in a one-bedroom apartment in the most rundown building in the neighborhood. The building looked like it belonged in a third world country. The blue paint was peeling off to reveal splintered and damaged wood. A metal slab covered the roof. The ground had shifted since the apartment had been built, creating a web of cracks in the walls and floor. Two bunk beds rested side by side in the living room and the space for a dining room table held a futon couch. To me, it looked like a nightmare, being crammed right next to your family like that. But these children were the happiest, most fun and loving kids you could ever want to meet. All of them were extremely polite and well mannered. The girls had an endless supply of hugs and laughed all day long. All of the children were very smart and made sure to do their homework and study for tests. Well, except for Mari Elena. She liked to play too much and got away with it because she was the youngest. The parents were incredibly devoted to their children and poured out their love and support.

 I had always heard that money doesn't matter and that things don't matter and it sounded so nice and proper that I wanted to believe it, even convincing myself that I did. But then the money that I had and the luxuries I possessed tugged at me to the point where it was hard to imagine being truly happy without them. I got to see the beauty and joy of simplicity played out right before my eyes and it was wonderful. For even a brief moment, the idea that I don't need anything other than what I already have is a relief. It is so difficult to live in a state of contentment and get rid of the desire to consume.

 Community life was quite an experience for all of us. Thankfully, I had lived with three roommates during my last two years of college, so I was used to sharing one bathroom between four women. Not only did we have to get used to living with seven other people of different backgrounds and cultures, but our home was the hot spot for kids all over the neighborhood, and sometimes a girl just wants some peace and quiet.

The eight of us shared a washer and dryer along with five women who had been city dwellers the previous year and now lived down the street. You had to time your laundry just so, because the kitchen in the community house became mobbed with kids. One day, I got distracted in the midst of washing my clothes and had to leave for one reason or another. I came home late that evening to find my clothes spread across the kitchen table for all to see. I gathered them into my basket with an eerie feeling that they might not have been alone this entire time.

That evening, I got a call from Nancy, one of the former city dwellers, asking me if I had been doing laundry at the community house earlier. I said that I had and wondered why she was asking. Nancy informed me that she came into the kitchen to find Irwin, one of the high school boys, running around and waving a tennis racket with a red thong draped over the end. She assured me that she confiscated it before they could put the rest of my underwear on their heads and run around the neighborhood. Note to self: do not leave laundry unattended.

I learned many other lessons the hard way. Thankfully, we had a safe place that was specifically for working out our difficulties. Once a week, the eight of us piled into two cars and headed out to Pasadena for an hour and a half of group therapy. I was skeptical at first, because I had been in therapy before and it was not the least bit helpful. I also wondered whether we would be able to be completely honest with each other and confront issues when they arose.

The first part of the session was a check in. We each had to use an adjective that described how we were feeling. Fine and good did not count. Our therapist, Sue, provided us with a long list of feeling words that we kept in the car and studied on the way to session. I drove the Buick and Christine drove her car, the person riding shotgun (usually Scott) was in charge of the radio, and one person in the back (usually Bobby) read off the list of adjectives. Some days I was sullen, other days I was frustrated, but most days I was joyful, my equivalent of fine.

The rest of the therapy time was open for bringing up issues. Dyhanne spent most of therapy braiding her hair, while Bobby and I looked at each other and giggled. Abel stared out the window, and Neil sat up straight, ready and eager for someone to break the silence. Neil and I couldn't let the silence go on for very long, so we usually chimed in, even if we didn't really have an issue to bring up.

The therapy did actually end up being helpful, because once we got used to it, people began to use the space to work out issues with other members of the team. It became a bit annoying to hear the boys arguing over the dishes session after session. There were other, more serious items addressed, but it was all confidential. I can hardly remember what they were anymore, which is funny, because at the time it seemed so dramatic.

In addition to having group therapy, we had a business meeting every Monday morning, led by Dan. We complained about those boring meetings, but in what other profession can you roll out of bed, saunter down the stairs in your pajamas and join your co-workers who have gathered in the living room. During one particular business meeting, Bobby excused himself to use the bathroom. We kept on discussing the agenda, and when Bobby came back to the group, he informed us that he had had a revelation while in the bathroom. We all laughed and thought he was joking, but Bobby continued with his grand idea. "What do you guys think about having a community worship service?" Bobby explained that we could plan a service in both English and Spanish where we could all worship God together. Everybody was excited about the idea, and the next time someone went to the bathroom during the meeting, we expected that person to return with a fabulous idea for a fundraiser.

Our first neighborhood worship was prepared and led by Fritze, Bobby and myself, as well as two women from the neighborhood. About twenty-five of us gathered in the living room of the community house to sing songs, read scripture, and pray together, all in English and Spanish. After the service, we shared a meal together.

It was a very powerful and beautiful experience to worship God in two languages with people who went to different churches, Catholic and Protestant. The Spanish speakers did their best to sing along in English and the English speakers did their best with the Spanish songs. We all appreciated the effort of the other to participate and seek unity despite the language barrier.

Six years later, the community house hosts what is now called "family night" once every two months, all because Bobby went to the bathroom and had a great idea.

Mexico

One of the most powerful experiences my city dweller year was a trip to Tijuana, Mexico. The point of the trip was to give us some insight into the lives of our neighbors. Growing up in San Diego, I had been to Tijuana many times, so I thought I knew what to expect. I had no idea that this trip would have such a profound effect on my view of the world.

The first part of our trip began at the border in San Ysidro, California. We met with Steve, a border patrol agent. Steve showed us a weapon in the war on illegal immigration. This device was heat sensitive and was able to detect the motion of people crossing the mountainous terrain between California and Mexico. We saw video footage of a small group of unsuspecting people traveling in the pitch black. The device the agents used made all of the people appear white, a stark contrast against the night sky. Suddenly, more white images riding horses appeared onto the screen, surrounding the group. We watched in awe as the white figures dove to the ground and stopped moving. The people were handcuffed and eventually returned to Mexico. I knew that many people tried to come to the United States from Mexico, but watching that video opened my eyes to both sides of the immigration issue.

The agent then took us to the border where Mexico and California meet at the Pacific Ocean. A concrete wall juts out into the water, but someone could easily swim around it.

The concrete wall continues on land and stands about ten feet tall. There is about 15 feet of open space between this wall and a chain link fence, behind which lies Mexico. Our group stared out at the metal fence and caught the glances of people peering back at us from the other side. It felt very strange to be fifty feet from these people, yet worlds away. I could sense them coveting our position and longing to be on our side of the fence. I had so many mixed emotions as I stared across at the people looking back at me. I wondered at the mystery of why some are born privileged while others are born into poverty. As I stood there, I prayed and questioned God about how He chooses who will be born on what side of the border. He didn't answer, but I felt encouraged to keep asking and seeking. Questions like these can cause serious doubt as to God's nature and even His existence. It is times like these that I have learned throughout my life that I need to trust in His goodness when life doesn't make sense to my limited knowledge of the world, and know that His wisdom and purpose is beyond my human ability to grasp.

Finally, our group crossed the border into Tijuana and headed out of the city onto dirt roads. We passed tattered shacks, mangy dogs, and children playing on our way to Iglesia Presbyteriana (the Presbyterian Church). We arrived after our off road experience in the Hollywood Presbyterian Church van, stepped outside and were immediately covered by dust. Efrain, the pastor, came out to greet us. He was very friendly and made us feel welcome. We had a little while to relax inside the church before the congregation was to join us for dinner. Each of us took our own pew and stretched out. Actually, I think Abel went exploring, as was his custom, while the rest of us crashed.

One by one, parents and children began to fill the little church.

The hum of conversation grew louder with each passing moment. Our group was a little bit shy, and only a few of us spoke Spanish, so we didn't make a big effort to mix in. The eight of us hovered together, a little overwhelmed in this new environment.

After dinner, Dan got up and announced that we were going to play a game together. I rolled my eyes and looked over at Scott, who was doing the same. Dan asked everybody to move the chairs into a big circle. The game was called tic-toc, which I had never heard of and immediately assumed to be stupid and boring. The first part of the game required us to go around the circle and say our names. There were about fifty people in the circle, forty one of whom I had never met, so there was no way I was going to remember all of those names. Dan then attempted to explain the game in Spanish and in English. One person was going to be "it" in the middle of the circle and they would point to someone and say "tic" and then to the next person and say "toc." It was a lot like duck, duck, goose. If the person in the middle stopped in front of you instead of continuing on around the circle, the pressure was now on that person. If they pointed to you and said tic, you had five seconds to say the name of the person on your right. If they pointed at you and said toc, you had five seconds to say the name of the person on your left. If you could not come up with the correct name in time, you would have to switch places with the person in the center. In addition to tic and toc, there was another word that could be used when the person in the center stopped in front of someone. This word was elefante. The person who was it could point at anyone they chose and say, "elefante." The chosen person would then have to stand up and put their arms out in front of them like the trunk of an elephant. The people on either side would have to stand up as well, lean toward the victim and position their arms in a circle to make elephant ears. Finally, the last option was for the person in the middle to shout out, "revolucion." Everybody would then have to get up and find a different chair. The person left without a chair was stuck in the middle.

I can't remember laughing so hard in a game as I did when we played this in Mexico. We were like children playing that game and

I felt a taste of the innocence I once had as a little girl. Every time three people had to make like an elephant, we would howl with laughter. When someone would yell "revolucion," a mad panic swept through us as we fought for that open seat, sometimes winding up in a stranger's lap. Every time we switched seats and sat next to a new person, we had to quickly get their name and memorize it as if our lives depended on it. We would watch as the person in the center stopped in front of a little old church lady and said toc. She would squint her eyes and pound her head trying to recall the name of a strange American. One of us would lean over and whisper in her ear, and the lady would repeat it just before the five seconds were up.

The silly game got us all interacting and having fun. The differences of socio-economic status and race that once seemed so pronounced drifted away. In this little church, we were simply God's children, enjoying one another's company and glorifying Him.

Later that evening, after we had all calmed down, our team split up into two groups and each group went to visit the home of a church member. My group walked about two blocks to the home of Manuel and Isabel. I was nervous because I knew that these people were very poor and I didn't want to appear shocked or stare rudely. I think for many people, myself included, that being face to face with someone who is extremely poor, terminally ill, physically handicapped, or facing any number of challenging obstacles, brings about fear and anxiety. What if they are unhappy? Will I be able to live the way I always have, knowing that people are poor and suffering? What if they are happy? Will my character be threatened because I am not up against such adversity? What do I say to them? What could I possibly have to say to someone in a situation that most people avoid like the plague? I felt the same way facing a family in poverty, as I would have felt going to the home of a quadriplegic: completely inadequate.

We entered the two-room house and my heart was in my stomach. Manuel led us to the couch and pulled up a couple of chairs from the table that sat in the middle of the room. I sat down and looked around the home. The floor was cement and the ceiling looked like a metal slab thrown over the walls of the house. Manuel set our minds at ease by initiating the conversation so that we wouldn't have to stumble around for words. He began by telling us about the family members who live in the home. There were nine people who inhabited the house, five children, two grandparents, and Manuel and his wife. I thought to myself that this was impossible. The house only had one main room apart from the kitchen, and there was a dining room table right in the middle of the room. Manuel informed us that they push the table against the wall at night and then pointed to some mats rolled up in the corner that were used as beds.

Manuel then began to share his faith with us. I had never before encountered a person as humble and in love with God who didn't have a worldly possession to his name. His was faith in the purest sense; when God is all you have and God is all you need. Manuel inspired me to desire God more than the material things that I often run to first. He caused me to look at the amount of stuff in my life that is extravagant and unnecessary. One of the goals of the city dweller program is to teach the discipline of a life of simplicity and Manuel was the perfect teacher.

Again, I was forced to address my feelings of superiority due to the color of my skin and the size of my bank account. The scripture verse that says, "Those who are first will be last and those who are last will be first," kept ringing in my ears. A life of simplicity gave Manuel a humility that was radiant, a faith that was firm and a sense of gratitude that was moving. My years of accumulating had only brought me an unsettled feeling of wanting more, an attitude of judgment, and a fleeting need for God.

We spent the night on the floor of the church, rolled up in sleeping bags. We were all exhausted and emotionally drained. I curled myself into a little ball to keep warm and played back the days events in my mind. Tears rolled down my face as I imagined Manuel and his family lying on their mats like sardines. I knew that I wanted to live my life differently, to be passionate about issues of poverty, to walk along side people who suffer. Nothing else in the world seemed to be as important or necessary.

I find myself realizing how much the desire and conviction I once held so dearly has faded without my realizing it. The hustle and bustle of life takes over and my priorities change to more self-centered goals such as school and work. Of course those things are important, but so is a little perspective.

I still struggle with materialism and the idea that "more is better." I live with one foot standing in the abundance and wealth of Hollywood and the other is standing in solidarity with the poor. How quickly and easily I forget the joy of simplicity when my desire to be noticed is the height of importance.

English as a Second Language

One of the jobs I signed up for my city dweller year was teaching English as a second language. I had never taught before, but this subject was close to my heart because I knew what it felt like to live in a foreign country and not speak the language.

My family moved to Spain when I was twelve years old because my parents are cool like that. They thought it would be a good idea for Derek and me to learn Spanish and experience a culture different from our own. My dad took a year's leave-of-absence from teaching Latin so that our family could go on an adventure together.

I was excited that they were finally letting us in on the fun, because I grew up hearing about their eighteen-month honeymoon in Europe where they rode my dad's motorcycle from country to country, camping and living on tomato and cheese sandwiches. After that, they spent a year in Australia where my mom worked in an orphanage and my dad worked at a motorcycle shop. Once they reached their late 20's, they settled down and did what most people do: get a job (in my dad's case, teaching) and have children.

My brother and I were enrolled in the only public school in our little town, San Lorenzo De El Escorial, and neither of us spoke a word of Spanish. We had only been in Spain a month before school started, so needless to say, Derek and I were a bit terrified. My dad gave us each a piece of paper that contained phrases such as, "Where is the bathroom?"

The timing of this trip couldn't have been better for me because I was twelve going on twenty one, and junior high in the states would have been a dangerous place for me. I idolized Madonna, wore dangly earrings, applied obnoxious amounts of blue eye shadow and wore mini skirts. My hair was put perfectly in its place with the help of a little Aqua Net, and I was not about to do anything that might mess it up. Growing up was all that was on my mind and the days of playing and getting dirty were long gone.

On the first day of school, I got up early, fixed my hair and makeup just so and slipped into the cutest skirt and sleeveless top I owned. Derek and I walked from our apartment complex, climbed over a concrete wall, and nervously ascended the steps to Antonio Rrobles, our new school. As we reached the hallway and it was time to separate, I wanted to pick Derek up, put him in my pocket and take him with me. Instead, I clutched my piece of paper and headed to the seventh grade classroom. The teacher greeted me and I responded by smiling and nodding, something I learned to do very well. Dona Maria led me to my seat and handed me some paper and a book. I looked around the room and noticed that I looked about five years older than all of the other kids. None of the girls were wearing makeup or skirts and most of them even wore sweats. I slid down into my seat and brushed my hand over my lips, removing the pink gloss. At recess, I learned that girls run around and play instead of checking out the boys and trying to look cool. I realized that I might have to reevaluate my wardrobe and grooming habits.

Twelve year olds are quite impressionable and will do anything to fit in, even wearing their hair in a ponytail and lacing up tennis shoes.

And do you know what I found out? I learned that playing tag and riding bikes is much more fun than checking my nails for dirt and my eyes for runny mascara. In Spain, I received what most kids in our country lose so early, a childhood.

Derek and I learned Spanish very quickly and by Christmas time, we were able to use words instead of hand gestures. We began to speak Spanish at home, rather than English, and shopkeepers would stare at the strange blonde family who had grown unusually tall and spoke to each other with an accent.

The memories I have from that year in Spain are some of the most vivid and wonderful of my childhood. Smells and colors and tastes from sixteen years ago fill my mind. All of my senses can be called upon to bring me back to the sweet chill of *leche merengada* on my tongue, the sting of flames lurching toward me during the festival of Las Fallas, or the rush of excitement at first laying eyes upon a magnificent castle. My family took trips all over Spain in our little blue Fiat. In the summer, Derek and I had to peel our selves off the vinyl seats in a rush to jump out and explore a new city.

Most precious to me are the memories of my family being together. My mom read *The Chronicles of Narnia* to Derek and me as we lay in front of the fireplace and watched the snow decorate our balcony. We took hikes together in the mountains above our home, where we even planted our Christmas tree. On Thanksgiving, my parents took us out of school early and we went into Madrid to celebrate at Burger King. I loved being with my family and even got along well with Derek (we didn't start fighting until high school). Many of the distractions that keep families from spending time together were absent in our new home. While so many junior high kids try and avoid being seen with their family, especially their parents, I loved every minute of our time together.

I have very fond feelings toward the Spanish people and culture. I dream about living half of the year over there and half of the year in Los Angeles. If it were financially feasible, I would do it in a second.

Teaching ESL turned out to be the most difficult job I have ever done. It took every ounce of patience I possessed and stretched me beyond what I thought I was capable of doing.

My class met in the living room of the community house and there were five women who came on a consistent basis. The woman with the most education had finished the second grade in Mexico. My students were eager to learn and excited to have the opportunity to go to school. On the first day of class, I asked each of the women why it was important to them to learn English. All of their responses were the same. They wanted to be able to help their children with their homework. I found this endearing and indicative of the hope immigrant family's place on the future of their children.

HUP did not have an ESL curriculum in place, so I made one up as I went along. This proved to be very challenging. The women in my class did not speak any English whatsoever. Because they did not have grammatical training in their own language, the whole idea of conjugating a verb was new to them. I had to teach my students how to conjugate verbs in Spanish before moving on to English. Every week, I had a new set of vocabulary words to teach, but the women would forget the words from the previous week. I tried to use matching games by placing the English words on one side of the page and the Spanish words in a different order on the other half of the page. To me, the activity was a simple concept that needed no explanation. The women were baffled and couldn't figure out what they were supposed to do with the words. I tried to explain that you draw a line from the English word to the matching Spanish word, but they looked at me as if I was trying to teach calculus.

I had never realized the importance of learning how to learn. These women did not know basic concepts of piecing information together that you learn all through out elementary school. Everything was new to them, from the basic structure of grammar, to simple testing measures. My heart went out to my students as I saw how difficult it was for them to make sense of what I was teaching. I realized how much I had taken for granted in my life and the simple luxury of a grammar school education.

We did the same lesson almost every day for the whole year. The women would be able to say sentences and identify words in class, but as soon as they went home, all of the knowledge drifted away. I felt like I was in the movie *Groundhog Day*, where Bill Murray experiences the same day over and over. That was my class, the same lesson day after day. My patience would run down my throat and through my stomach, head toward my legs and start to make a run for the door. It took everything in me not to give up. It was hopeless. These women were never going to learn the words for eggs or milk or corn. They were never going to be able to help their children write sentences or identify nouns.

I was baffled as to why they came back every day. I was sure that one day, they would figure out that I was a phony teacher who was at her wit's end, and decide to play hooky for the rest of the year. But even though they were not learning enough English to communicate or even say a few words, they were dedicated and faithful. These women were not about to give up. It made me feel proud and guilty and frustrated all at once.

Finally, after months of frustration, I decided that we were going to do the same lesson every day and that was going to be okay. I realized that these women were gaining a sense of dignity and they actually felt like they were achieving something. Who was I to say that they were not learning anything? And it turns out that in the end, they were the ones who taught me. I may have been able to speak English and Spanish fluently, but they had experience under their belts that outweighed anything I could have gained from books and studies.

The women were so grateful for the English classes, that they often invited me to their homes for dinner. HUP does not charge anything for the classes, and the women wanted to give something back. I gladly accepted, feeling a little guilty because my teaching skills really did not warrant a home cooked meal.

My most outspoken student, Amelia, was the first to invite me to her apartment. She lived three blocks away from the community house, in a one-bedroom apartment with her husband and three children. I arrived at her place right on time at 5 o'clock, which actually turns out to be at least an hour early in the Latino culture. I quickly learned that if the invitation says the party starts at 3 o'clock and goes until 9 o'clock, people usually show up at six and stay until the wee hours of the morning.

Amelia led me into her home and pulled out a chair for me at the dining room table. I looked around the apartment and saw the familiar decoration that I had grown accustomed to seeing in the homes of my neighbors. The wall held 8x10 school pictures of the children in their uniforms of white shirts and blue shorts. There were also several pictures of Jesus, some of him on the cross and one where he was holding a lamb. Mixed in between Jesus and the children was a large ornamental decoration made of wood and colorful knitted material that read, "Recuerdo de Mexico." The couches were covered with bed linens, and the shelves that held the television were adorned with little porcelain figurines, so that none of the wood on the top shelf was visible.

I sat at the table and soaked in all that made Amelia's home uniquely hers. She was stirring a big, boiling pot of mystery food. I was a little bit nervous because Bobby had been invited to a neighbor's house for dinner and ate some sort of soup. He found out afterward that the soup had a cow's hoof marinating in it. Yum. It may have been quite delicious, but I was skeptical and was desperately hoping Amelia was cooking chicken.

As my eyes moved from the living room back to the kitchen, I noticed roaches, big and small, scaling the wall and the countertops freely. Amelia paid them no attention, so I tried not to stare. Amelia broke the silence and began to share with me about her life. She became the teacher, and I was the eager student. I am afraid I learned more that night than I was able to teach her in one year. Amelia's story has profoundly impacted my life and it challenges me to seek new depths of honor in my own character. I feel that my life is now entwined with hers in a precious memory to call upon when life feels insignificant and hopeless. Hers is a story of courage beyond anything I could muster in myself, so I draw from her life as an example of true sacrifice and love.

Amelia grew up in a rural town in Mexico, with ten brothers and sisters. The boys in her family were able to go to school until they were twelve years old, but Amelia and her sisters were put to work as soon as they turned seven. The steam from the mystery soup danced around her face as she recalled these memories. Amelia did not realize that she was poor, though she didn't have any shoes and was only fed rice, beans and corn every day. She recalled being joyful as a child, clinging to innocence even though she was out in the fields working.

Amelia married at age fifteen and had her first child at sixteen. She and her husband and brand new baby were forced to move into the city because work was sparse. Her husband found a job working long and labor intensive hours in a factory. The pay was close to nothing and Amelia would skip meals in order to feed her baby. A few years later, another baby followed. Even though Amelia knew that things would be difficult financially, she was overjoyed at being pregnant. She adored her son and lived her life in service to her children and her husband. As Amelia revealed her life history, there was never a hint of regret or anger. I remember sitting at that table and thinking that Amelia was pregnant with her second child and living in a shack at age 18, while I was off at college, occasionally studying, but mostly partying. It was amazing to me that we had been thrown together at this time in our lives, and funny that our lives should intersect at all.

Amelia continued with her fascinating life history. She became pregnant yet again two years after the second child was born. During this time, the economy was growing worse and people were getting laid off at the factory. Amelia's husband, Juan, lost his job in the second round of lay offs. He searched for another job, but nobody was hiring. He arrived home one evening after searching for work all day and brought up the idea of trying to cross the border to America. Juan had a cousin who lived in Los Angeles that would take them in. Amelia was scared to leave her home country and all that was familiar, but she knew that her children would have more opportunity in America. Pregnant with two young children, Amelia decided to make the journey with the hope of a brighter future for her kids.

Juan found a coyote (someone who is hired to lead people across the border illegally) that had helped some friends he knew cross the border through the rough terrain. The trip would take about a week, traveling by night and keeping hidden during the day. The coyote warned them of the risks, little food and water, exhausting conditions, and the danger of being caught and returned home. Amelia and Juan's dreams of living in America outweighed the risks, so they paid the coyote what little money remained.

Amelia described the trip to me as I sat in her kitchen, watching the roaches crawl this way and that. At times, she was so tired of walking that she wanted to quit and stay behind to die. Her husband helped her and carried the children on his back, one at a time. Amelia kept going at the thought of making it across safely and giving birth to her third child, who would be an American citizen.

The nights were bitter cold, but the children did not cry. Amelia could sense that they knew the importance of staying quiet. It was difficult to make their way through the brush at night, navigating frozen toes through the pitch dark. Frequently, the sound of someone tripping and crashing to the ground interrupted the soft shuffle of feet. In the distance, the hum of a helicopter could be heard and everyone dove to the ground, not moving an inch until the noise had long faded. The sound of heavy breathing filled the air, a combination of exhaustion and fear.

During the day, their group sought shelter in the heavy brush. They lay still and waited for the moon, swallowed whole by dry leaves. The coyote warned them not to eat the berries that had come to look like a heavenly feast. Their stomachs had stopped growling by the third day, succumbing to the reality that they would not be filled.

In addition to her family, there were seven other people in the group. They knew each other purely by sight; no words had passed between them. But she could see that familiar look in their eyes, the one that hoped for a new life. Those seven strangers became her companions, and all the things that remained unspoken were clearly understood between them. She couldn't think of any words that captured all of the feelings of that time, nothing but silence seemed fit.

After six days of travel, Amelia and her family were safely across the border. They headed down the desolate hills and made their way into the city of San Diego. They had written to Juan's cousin to let him know they were coming. As soon as they were able, Juan called his cousin and he drove down from Los Angeles to pick them up.

Four months later, Amelia gave birth to a baby boy, Antonio, an American citizen. Juan got a job as a painter, working a few days a week as needed. The family was able to move to Hollywood into their own apartment and begin living in this new culture, where language and customs and values were so different from what they had always known. The two older children were enrolled in school and began to learn English very quickly. Amelia was often homesick for familiar places and the company of friends, but she found many people in her neighborhood with stories similar to her own. Amelia has now adapted to life in America, and is grateful that she made the journey. She believes that her children have many more opportunities here, and her life is dedicated to ensuring their success.

Neighborhood Youth

In addition to teaching English, I spent the rest of my city dweller year working with youth from the neighborhood. The youth became such an important part of my life that I could not imagine leaving them at the end of the year. When my internship ended, I decided to make my home in the neighborhood. Christine and I moved into our own apartment a block away from the community house. My life had been so touched by these kids and I wanted to watch them grow and mature, giving encouragement and helping them through the trials of high school.

My friend, Nancy, and I coached a volleyball team for two years. The highlight for the teenage boys was riding to practice and games in the Buick. There was always a fight for shotgun and control of the radio. Power 106 was the station of choice and we cruised down Wilshire with the bass pumping, windows rolled down and hands hanging out, moving up and down with the rhythm. Other motorists would glare at me for subjecting them to the musical stylings of Snoop Doggy Dogg and Tupac.

When we first started the volleyball team, only two of the girls had ever played volleyball before. The high school boys would pick up the white leather balls during practice and nail them at each other. It took us a while to convince them that volleyball was a very different sport than dodgeball. The first few weeks of practice were like a war zone with balls flying everywhere. Once we finally convinced them to quit trying to kill each other and learn how to play the game, volleyball practice became one of the most enjoyable parts of my week.

The real test came when we started playing against other teams. Our kids were so scared at the beginning of the first game that none of them wanted to play. The other team had taken their position behind the net and was waiting for their opponents. Nancy and I tried to reassure them, but they looked at us like we were asking them to go into combat. It was slightly amusing to see these kids quivering in the corner, because they usually acted like nothing could possibly scare them. The referee came over and asked the kids to take the court. Reluctantly, they set up in the format that they had learned in practice.

The referee threw the ball to a girl from the other team and blew the whistle. The girl tossed the ball in the air and banged it over the net. Our team watched as the ball hit the floor between two of our guys who had actually moved out of the way. After the other team had served five aces in a row, Tony finally stepped up when the ball came his way and hit it back over the net. The kids on our bench went wild, and the kids on the court ran over to give him a high five just as the other team hit the ball back over and it dropped to the empty backcourt.

In the moment that Tony hit the ball back over the net, our kids experienced the thrill of competition and accomplishment. The look of fear washed away from their faces and was replaced with the look of determination and joy. We ended up getting beaten badly, but we did not give up and actually hit the ball back over the net several more times.

In that first season, we lost every single game we played. In our second season, we won one game by forfeit. Nancy and I could not have been more proud of those kids because they improved so much and began to give the other teams a run for their money.

Most importantly, the youth began to appreciate one another. The older kids looked after the younger ones and friendships blossomed. They learned to work together and rely on each other.

All three of the girls who competed on the volleyball team were also part of a Bible study that I co-led with another woman named Carrie. I met Carrie during my first month in Hollywood at a meeting for the HUP tutoring program. She had been a tutor the previous year as a volunteer from the First Presbyterian Church of Hollywood. At the meeting, Carrie mentioned that she would like to start a Bible study for teenage girls in the neighborhood. When I told her that I would be interested in working with her, she immediately attached herself to me. Carrie's warm personality came through in a Texas drawl, and it was a bit overwhelming. She is one of those nice people that make you feel like a jerk. This is not due to pretentiousness on her part, but simply because of the genuine kindness with which she treats everyone. As we were planning and making preparations for the Bible study, Carrie called me at least once a day, if not two or three times. Her voice was just so sweet, and she said things like "ya'll," so I couldn't show my annoyance, revealing that I am indeed a jerk.

Our first Bible study was planned for a warm Los Angeles Saturday in November. Carrie showed up at the community house 20 minutes late, holding two boxes of donuts. We sat on the floor of the house and watched the minutes tick by on the clock. After an hour, we decided to eat our share of the donuts and acknowledge that nobody was going to come. This occurred two more times, with Carrie showing up 20 minutes late and nobody coming in behind her.

It was time to re-group and get a different strategy. We came up with a plan to have a party instead of a Bible study. Teenage girls are probably more interested in going to parties than studying the Bible. This should be obvious, so I don't know why we didn't think of the idea sooner. It was nearing Christmas by this time, so a holiday party seemed perfect.

Five junior high and high school girls showed up at the community house the night of the party. We piled into the Buick and headed to Carrie's house in the Hollywood hills. The girls were a little shy at first, but after a few pieces of pizza, everybody started to loosen up. Carrie had a Christmas tree set up in her living room and our project for the evening was to decorate it. We had several boxes of cream colored ornaments and permanent markers. The first ornament was to contain our hopes and dreams, in words and pictures that wrapped around the ornament. When everyone was finished writing, we each shared what we had written. There is nothing like sharing your dreams with people to bond you together. Our dreams were everything from getting into college to becoming an actress. I knew from our time together that I wanted to journey along side the girls and my new friend Carrie as they lived in the face of those dreams. Our second ornament was decorated with things for which we were thankful. Our families, friends and health topped almost every list. At the end of the night, the tree was adorned in hope, aspiration, joy, thanksgiving and love.

The next time we attempted a Bible study, eight junior high and high school girls attended. The goal of this study was to share with the girls how deeply God loves them, and that they are precious to Him. In the months and years that followed, Carrie and I fell in love with them too.

Our Bible study had a theme song. In our second year, we were joined by a new city dweller named Cindy, who played the guitar and added music to our list of activities. The girls always asked to sing one song in particular, and we came to think of it as our theme song. The words are as follows:

How could anyone ever tell you that you are anything less than beautiful?
How could anyone ever tell you that you are less than whole?
How could anyone fail to notice that your loving is a miracle?
How deeply you're connected to my soul.

We would sing this song three times. The first time, we would sing it to each other. The second time, we would sing it to Jesus. The third time, we would imagine that Jesus was singing it to us. I often had to fight to keep the tears from welling up in my eyes when we sang our song together.

I have many fond memories of summer camp, slumber parties, movie nights, and trips to McDonalds. Several of the girls were on their high school softball and volleyball teams, and I went to cheer as often as I could. I thought my heart might jump out of my chest as I looked out to see them waving at me from the field in the middle of the game.

Our group met almost once every week for the next three years. We endured painful trials and celebrated triumphs. In a neighborhood where dropping out of school is frequent, all of the high school girls graduated and some went on to college. My life will never be the same because of the things they taught me about how to love and how to persevere when the odds are stacked against you.

I have so many fond memories of the girls, but one Bible study in particular stands out above the rest. A month or so before this Bible study, two of the girls, Melissa and Carla, had come to talk to me about their best friend, Jessica. They were extremely worried about her, and told me that Jessica had become very depressed. Jessica had built many walls up around herself, unwilling to let people get too close. After two years, I still felt that she was not ready to completely trust me. I didn't know what else I could do or say to earn that trust. It was clear to me from the first time I met Jessica that her life had been one painful trial after another. It was written on her face and the way she carried herself. She was not carefree and lighthearted like the other girls. She was more cynical and guarded. Carrie, Cindy and I wanted so much for Jessica to allow us into her brokenness and to let us love her.

I told Melissa and Carla that I would have a talk with her, but in my heart, I did not think that she would open up to me. The next day, I walked to Jessica's apartment after school was out. The building was locked and I peeked in the kitchen window of her apartment where her mother, Isabel, happened to be getting a drink. Isabel yelled to Jessica to come and let me in. When she finally appeared in the doorway, I asked her if she would like to take a walk. Reluctantly, Jessica followed me down the street. She walked just a little bit behind me, and when I slowed down to walk along side her, she slowed down too. I asked Jessica about school and she gave the typical teenage response, "school is fine." Everything was fine. She did not have more than a two-word answer to any of my questions and it was clear that she had no intention of sharing what was really going on.

About a month after my failed attempt to get Jessica to open up, Cindy led a Bible study that none of us will ever forget. Jessica, Carla, Melissa, and a few other girls were in attendance. Cindy began the study by talking about the many ways that God is active in our lives. Then, she read from a little pamphlet called "God is." Cindy told us to close our eyes and listen to each phrase, noting the one that seemed most fitting to who God is in our lives right now. "God is my friend…God is my father…God is loving…God is a healer…God is compassionate…God is my redeemer…God is just…God is forgiving…God is faithful…God is my comfort…" We listened quietly as the list continued and I was struck by how little I recognize God in all these ways. When Cindy finished reading, she asked us if we would like to share the phrase that stood out to us. Melissa raised her hand and was the first brave person to share. She said, "My real father left my family when I was a baby and I never knew him. To me, God is my father." I wanted to take Melissa in my arms and hold onto her. She is such a gift, and I felt sad that her own father would never know how wonderful she is.

A few more people shared, and then there was a brief silence. Just as we were about to pray, Jessica nervously raised her hand. I looked over at her, eager to hear what she had to say, because she rarely spoke up during Bible study. Jessica looked down at the floor and took a deep breath before saying, "God is a healer." She paused again and took another breath. The room was silent and all eyes were on Jessica. She began to cry as she said, "Lately, I have been hurting myself and I don't know how to stop." She rolled up her sleeves to reveal hundreds of wounds up and down her arms. Scars had already developed and there were also fresh cuts on her forearms. Immediately, Melissa and Carla ran over and draped their arms around her. I could not keep my own tears inside as I looked at Jessica's arms, torn and mutilated. We all huddled together and cried, collectively expressing the pain of one of our own. Jessica had hidden her face in her palms and when she looked up to see us gathered around her, sobbing like babies, she began to laugh. I thought to myself, God is a healer, and I could see Him working in that very moment.

We held hands together and prayed, thanking God for being just what we need. The girls prayed for each other and I felt like a proud parent.

Our Bible study lasted for three years until most of the girls graduated and moved away. Whenever I am feeling down on myself, I imagine them singing to me, "how could anyone ever tell you that you are anything less than beautiful."

Animal Planet

I am not someone you would call an animal lover. In fact, I dislike most kinds of animals. I realize that I am in the minority on this subject, and that some people don't like people who don't like animals. I have given up trying to pretend that I think dogs are fun and cats are cute. I feel I need to place a warning on this chapter, at least for the PETA people, because you may not like what you are about to read.

I have tried to remember a traumatic experience from my childhood involving animals, and I can't think of anything. I have been scared of dogs for as long as I can remember, but I don't know why that is. I am also afraid of horses, particularly of riding them.

My Mom was not very sensitive to my phobia and signed my family up for a four-hour mule ride in Yosemite when I was at the tender age of 19. I tried to beg her to let me out of it, but it was her birthday and this was what she wanted to do. My parents assured me that I would be fine. I agreed to go along, only because it was my mom's birthday.

We mounted our mules and got in line behind the rest of the adventure-seeking tourists. At first, it wasn't bad. My mule, Ginger, followed along nice and slow behind the group. I was in the middle of the pack, which helped put me slightly at ease. There was an instructor at the very front and one at the back. All of a sudden, the path began to narrow and we started to ascend what looked to me like Mount Everest. The trail became about 2 feet wide and the mules tight roped up the steep incline. I refused to let myself look down. About half way up the mountain, Ginger stopped and did a 180-degree pirouette, and ended up facing the other mules headed upward. I started to panic and envisioned myself hurtling off the cliff to my death. Of course I would get the suicidal mule. The instructor yelled at me to turn the mule around. Who the hell did he think I was, John Wayne? There was very little room to maneuver and I couldn't imagine how I could get Ginger to turn around without flying off the trail. I just wanted to get off and walk back down to safety. The instructor would not let me abandon Ginger. He got off his mule and came up to turn Ginger around. We continued up the mountain and I bargained with God that I would be good the rest of my life if He would be so kind as to allow me to live through this. I whispered in Ginger's ear that she had much to live for and whatever was troubling her could be sorted out at the bottom of the mountain.

When the four-hour tour was up and I touched the ground safely, I wanted to bend down and kiss the dirt beneath me. My family thought it was the funniest thing they had ever seen and joked about my trauma. I vowed never to ride an animal again. I don't care whose birthday it is.

Hollywood provided me with plenty more opportunities to build on my dislike for animals. My city dweller year, the neighbors had a rooster that served as an unwanted alarm clock. I know that it sounds strange to have a rooster in the city, but there were all kinds of odd animals hanging around. Some neighbors had a goat that they cared for lovingly, feeding it to its heart's content. Who knew they were fattening it up for a feast of plenty. One day, the goat was gone and the neighbors were napping on the porch with full bellies. Several rabbits ran the streets, grazing on whatever bits of grass they could find.

An adolescent boy had a pet iguana that he walked around town on a leash. The dogs, however, were my biggest fear. Stray dogs wandered aimlessly, carrying rabies for sure. I would never make eye contact with them and slowly crossed to the opposite side of the street when I saw one approaching. There was one dog in particular that came to be my worst enemy. Sassy was the dog's name, and he was trapped safely in my next-door neighbors yard. I was not scared of this dog. He was a medium sized, yellow mutt, and some people might have even thought he was cute.

The problem with Sassy is that he barked and yelped and cried during the middle of the night. My window was right above his doghouse and he serenaded me all night long. I became sleep deprived, which led me to become very cranky. I tried to talk to Sassy's owners, but they denied ever hearing Sassy barking in the middle of the night. This made me even more frustrated because I knew I wasn't imagining things. Sometimes, I would walk downstairs at three o'clock in the morning, stand in front of the fence, and stare Sassy down. I thought maybe if he saw how tired I looked he would have pity and be quiet. No such luck. I dragged my sleepy butt back to bed and tossed and turned the rest of the night.

One evening, my sleep was disturbed yet again by that obnoxious barking. I was just about to go outside for another staring contest when I heard a window from the apartment below me violently slide open. A man's voice roared back at the dog. "Shut up. Shut the fuck up." Sassy kept right on barking and I fell back into bed laughing.

Mercifully, Sassy vanished one day. I didn't know if he ran away, died, or if the neighbors had gotten rid of him. Frankly, I didn't care, just as long as he was never coming back.

About a week after Sassy had been gone, there was a knock at my door. The little boy from next door was standing in front of me holding a piece of paper. He asked if I would sign a petition to get his dog back because it had been taken to the pound. I looked the boy right in his cute little face and told him that I couldn't sign the petition because his dog kept me awake at night. I know, that is the meanest thing anyone has ever done to a child. I am a horrible person. But I was so glad for the peace and quiet and for the brilliant person who complained and had the dog removed.

Not only were there animals wandering the streets, but there were also some in my apartment. We had your typical dwellers of inner-city apartments: mice and roaches. We had the apartment fumigated three times, and the roaches would return shortly after the bug killer left.

I wish somebody had video taped the first time Christine and I saw a mouse. We were both in the kitchen when we saw the little fur ball scamper across the floor and under the stove. We took off running for safety and jumped onto the couch, screaming like, well, girls. After a few minutes, Christine tiptoed back into the kitchen to scope out the situation. I stayed glued to the couch. A second later she screamed again and made a mad dash back to the couch.

This was a problem. I don't like animals, and mice are the worst kind. They are dirty and ugly and gross.

Christine and I headed to Sav On to buy some traps. We set them up throughout the kitchen and waited for them to do their job. After the first mouse was caught, we both looked at each and thought the same thing: What do we do now? Neither of us wanted to pick up the trap and throw it away. The only solution was to go down the street and find one of our friends to take care of the situation. HUP was having a board meeting and we camped outside the community house for a willing volunteer. Our friend Patrick agreed to come over. He walked into our kitchen, picked up the mouse as if it were a banana peel, and tossed it into the trash. Patrick was kind enough to take the trash with him when he left, because we didn't even want to touch the container that held the mouse.

Christine and I were in for a rude awakening, because Mickey had friends and family. The more we became accustomed to the little intruders, the less we were sent running for the couch. I started becoming very brave and was able to pick up the traps and discard the dead mice myself. Soon, I was chasing them around the kitchen with a frying pan and would have bashed them right on the head if I could have caught the suckers.

Right up there with my hatred for mice is my disdain for pigeons. They are hideous, worthless creatures in my opinion. I have my reasons for hating them. I might not care one way or the other about them if they hadn't invaded my balcony and set up shop. But those pigeons chose the wrong apartment and the wrong animal hater.

It would have been nice to put some lounge chairs and a barbecue on my balcony. I would have loved to cook hamburgers and hotdogs and then relax on a plastic chair, enjoying the view of the Hollywood sign. But that was not to be. My balcony was covered in bird crap. The pigeons swooped down, chased each other around for a while, crapped all over, and then flew off. Did you know that pigeons fight each other? They do. They are horrible, vicious animals. They peck at each other and fluff each other feathers, all the while making cooing and screeching noises that make me want to run for the hills. I would hear a thump against the sliding door as one bird pushed another into the glass. Christine informed me that the pigeons were actually mating, which made them seem even more barbaric.

I tried to combat the problem by purchasing a fake wooden owl that was supposed to scare the birds away. It worked for about a day. Pigeons aren't as dumb as you might think and they figured out that the owl never moved. They took to landing on its head and pushing it around during their fights.

The fruits of the birds' labor showed up one day as tiny little eggs nestled on some twigs and leaves that had been imported onto the balcony. The mother sat protectively on top of them, and I knew they were there to stay. It was my own private animal planet show. We watched as the mother cared for her unborn children by warding off other birds. We saw the two babies right after they had been born, shriveled and weak. They grew before our eyes, learning to feed themselves and flap their wings.

This was all very interesting and educational for sure, but I wanted my balcony back. I had plans to buy some fencing that I had seen at the Home Depot and construct a blockade to keep the birds out. I was losing my patience and kept coaxing them to fly away as I put my nose to the glass that separated us. The mother had abandoned them, and they looked big enough to fly. I decided it was time to take matters into my own hands and adopt the title, mama bird. I got a broom out of the closet and tentatively pushed open the glass door. I was very nervous and wondered if I had the guts to go through with my plan. I slid the door open enough to fit the broom through, yet keep myself protected behind the glass. I moved the broom toward one of the birds and gently pushed it. The bird pushed back and had no intention of being swept away. I closed my eyes and pushed a little harder until there was no more resistance. I quickly did the same with the other bird, then slammed the sliding door and fell onto the couch, my heart pounding. I felt guilty and cruel and relieved. I went downstairs and checked the grass below the balcony to see if I was a murderer. I cried out for joy when it became clear that I hadn't actually sent the birds to their death, but rather, had given them a flying lesson.

Christine and I set off for Home Depot and purchased the fencing. We came home and pigeon proofed our balcony. We scrubbed and cleaned and made ourselves ill on the fumes of bleach. When it was all done, we had reclaimed our balcony and the pigeons would have to find a tree to house their babies and a telephone wire to play on.

After that incident, I became a bit paranoid that while walking down the street, the pigeons I had sent flying would dive-bomb me. I was worried they would recognize me and say to each other, "hey, there's the bitch that tried to kill us. Let's get her." And then they would swoop down and peck at my head and crap all over me. Thankfully, that never happened.

Apartment #5

The eight-unit apartment complex that housed me and Christine and the mice and the roaches was also home to an interesting assortment of families and individuals. I have countless stories about my neighbors, but I will only describe a few of my favorites. Christine and I spent three long years in this building, and we had been there the longest of anybody by the time we left.

We all complained about our absent landlord, Art, who neglected his tenants and the run-down building. I am not an aggressive person, but I often wanted to bash Art's head in. He brought out an anger and frustration in me that few people have managed to elicit. We would often come home to find a notice from the gas company informing us that the bill had not been paid and our gas was going to be shut off. This meant that we would not have hot water. There was one period of time where we went for a month without hot water. I started going to the gym to take a shower, not to work out. The receptionist always looked at me funny when I would walk out with wet hair 20 minutes after coming in.

A lady named Virginia inhabited the apartment below us. She wanted to bash Art's head in too and probably could have done it with her bare hand. Virginia had two sons that came and went, as well as being the legal guardian of two grandchildren by her daughter. One of her sons was quite a character, and I have a story about him that I will tell later. The other son is the famous man who cussed out the barking dog across the street. He always wore fun and decorative hats that merited a second glance when people passed him on the street. The granddaughters were beautiful and athletic. They rode bikes and chased each other around the parking garage, sending out an echo of squeals and laughter, notifying the entire building that they were having the time of their lives. Most of Virginia's free time was spent smoking cigarettes on the balcony and yelling at her grandchildren down below.

The apartment building had a small downstairs garage where the children played and the most daring tenets parked their cars. I tried to park in there one time and scraped both sides of my car getting out. There was another parking area in the back alley, where Christine and I parked. I interrupted several drug deals in that alley, and I once had to wait for a homeless man to finish relieving himself and leave before I could pull into my parking place. The building itself was a faded green color that looked like vomit. Several large cracks sprouted up the front of the building like the San Andreas Fault. Our apartment did not have any heat, which you might not think would be a problem in L.A., but when it got down into the 40's during the winter, there was no difference between the temperature outside and the temperature in our apartment. Christine and I would sit on our couch, huddled together watching television wearing our winter coats, gloves, and scarves. Yes, it was a bit of a nightmare, but it was home.

Christine and I had both gone out of town one weekend only to come home and find that the toilet in my bathroom had been flooding for two days. The carpet in my bedroom was completely soaked and had ruined my furniture. The weight of the water had caused the ceiling in Virginia's bedroom to cave in and chunks of plaster began to fall on her in the middle of the night. She had tried to call Art all weekend with no response. I called him as soon as I got home and left several messages.

Art sent someone to fix Virginia's ceiling and my toilet one week later. By this time, the apartment reeked of mildew and the carpet was mostly dry. I threatened Art in the nicest possible Christian way that he better send someone out to clean and disinfect the carpet or he could expect to receive a call from my lawyer. I mean, my dad.

The neighbors directly across from us were another challenge to my patience and sanity. Actually, my only problem was with the sixteen-year-old boy, Cheto. He was a little punk who insisted on playing his rap music loud enough for the whole neighborhood to hear. The door of the apartment was always left open; to make sure that everybody in the vicinity was subjected to the noise. Among his favorite songs were, *Fuck the Police* and an explicit song about a girl getting raped. I tried to ask Cheto in my friendliest voice to please turn the volume down or at least close the door. He would turn the volume down a few notches, so that the people four buildings down could no longer hear it, but I was still in misery.

It was time to fight back, and I had just the CD to do it with. My evangelistic friend Carrie had given me a CD with the most popular Christian worship music. I popped in the CD and turned up the volume as high as it would go. I waged war against *Fuck the Police* with *Lord, I Lift Your Name on High*. My door was propped open and the battle was under way. Cheto folded and the sound of his footsteps on the stairs was music to my ears. Victory. I turned off the CD and gloated in the silence. My strategy never failed. Every time I couldn't take the rap music anymore, I put in my CD and it worked like magic.

Late one evening, I was at home relaxing and watching television. All of a sudden I heard the popping sound of gunshots, one after the other. I dove to the ground, startled, even though I was on the second floor. After the shooting stopped, the door across from me slammed and I heard the familiar sound of feet running down the stairs. I looked out the window to make sure nobody had been hit, and saw Cheto jump into the car that had fired the shots. The tires screeched as the car peeled out of site.

Thankfully, there weren't any victims. I could hear Virginia downstairs cursing. A bullet had struck her balcony, and I thought she might run off down the street after the car, waving her broom. I called the police to report the incident and they said someone would be out shortly to investigate. A police car pulled up forty-five minutes later. If the same incident had happened six blocks away in Hancock Park where the rich people live in their multi-million dollar homes, you can bet that the cops would have been there in minutes.

Downstairs, at the back end of the building, lived a sweet lady named Maria. The apartment that she shared with her daughter was covered from top to bottom in furniture, pictures, and an assortment of junk. Maria is one of those people who can't throw anything away. She is also one of those people who love to chitchat. Whenever I ran into her, she could keep me for as long as thirty minutes discussing everything from the weather, to her dead husband. One of her favorite people was Christine, and Maria would hold her captive in conversation as well. An avid gardener in a city of concrete, Maria kept a fine assortment of potted plants, which she proudly displayed on the downstairs walkway. Those shrubs were watered faithfully and pampered like children.

Downstairs and across from Virginia's apartment, lived an immigrant family from Mexico. There were two parents and two sons. They lived in a one-bedroom apartment, so the living room had a bed next to the couch. The father, Ramon, was friendly and outgoing, as were the two boys, Benito and Jose. The mother was quiet and meek and I don't think I heard her speak three sentences in three whole years. Ramon affectionately gave me the nickname, "huera," which means white girl in Spanish. He would yell at me from downstairs, "Huera, quieres carne asada?" Ramon was very generous with the carne asada that he barbecued and was offended if I didn't try it. He savored the look on my face when I bit into the meat, closed my eyes and let the spices thrill my tongue.

A few weeks before Christine and I moved out of the building to a house down the street, I had a yard sale. Ramon came out at ten in the morning to find me sitting behind my dining room table, surrounded by odds and ends that I was getting rid of. "Huera, why didn't you tell me you were having a yard sale?" he asked in Spanish. He acted as if I was having a party and didn't invite him. It turns out this is exactly what he thought. He went right on down to the 7-11 and bought a 12 pack of corona for the occasion. While he was gone, Maria, the plant lady, came out to investigate the treasures. She sat down in one of the chairs and began talking a mile a minute. Ramon came back with his purchase and offered us each a beer. This quieted Maria right down as she grabbed the bottle and examined the contents, debating whether or not to drink it. I could tell that she didn't really want it but she sipped the corona delicately, barely wetting her lips and set it back on the table. I have never acquired a taste for beer, and I especially was not tempted at ten o'clock in the morning. "Mas para mi (more for me)," said Ramon with a hearty laugh.

We sat around the table talking and laughing, ignoring the bargain hunters who sifted through boxes and held up porcelain cups to the sun, checking for cracks. Ramon's wife came out of the apartment briefly to see what he was up to, and as soon as we made eye contact, she looked down shyly and headed back inside.

Maria kept mentioning how comfortable the chairs were. She got up and tried out all four of them, nudging Ramon out of his seat as he grumbled and threw his arms up in the air, annoyed about being displaced. Every time Maria sat down, she would sink into the chair and say, "ahhhh." Maria is a heavy-set woman with back problems and has trouble finding chairs that she fits in comfortably. Maria decided that she definitely needed to buy the dining room table and chairs. In my mind, I saw her already crammed apartment and wondered where she would possibly have room for them. I kept the table at my place for two days until she had created enough space in her apartment, but the chairs were taken straight to their new home. All of the floor space was already used up, so I imagine the chairs ended up on top of the bed.

One day, as I arrived home from work, a homeless man was sitting on the steps leading up to the building, smoking a cigarette. I was going to sneak around him quickly, so as not to disturb him. Actually, it was more because I didn't want him to disturb me. His hair was dirty and ratted, and his jeans had holes that were not the result of a fashion statement. The neck of his sweater was stretched out enough to reveal his shoulder.

As I was about to make a graceful move around him, he stood up right in front of me and I got a big whiff of smoke and body odor. He reached out his hand to me and introduced himself as Virginia's son, Mike. "My name is Mandy," I replied, and placed my palm in his.

"Mandy. That is such a beautiful name."

I thanked him and had to remove my hand from his grasp with a bit of force. As I made my way up the stairs to my apartment, I could feel him watching me, and it made me nervous. I wasn't nervous in the damsel in distress type way, because I pride myself on the fact that my height and athleticism would deter most would-be attackers. I had a good five inches and 15 pounds on Mike, so it really wouldn't be a contest in my opinion. He made me nervous in the way that some men are just creepy.

The following day, I came home from work to find Mike in the exact same spot on the stairs, soaking up the sun. He was wearing the same clothes as the day before. I was hoping that he wouldn't sense my presence, since his eyes were closed. I tried to tip toe past, but he jumped up with his hand extended. "Hi, I'm Mike. What's your name?"

"Mandy" I replied, a little confused.

"Oh, that's a beautiful name. It's nice to meet you Mandy."

"It's nice to meet you too," I said hesitantly. *I must not be very memorable*, I thought.

The same scenario played out every time I encountered Mike in the next few days. He never remembered that we had met and that he had already told me that my name was beautiful.

After Mike had been hanging around the building for a week or so, he began to act even more strange. Instead of saying hi, he stared at me with a wild look in his eyes. Mike paced back and forth, talking to himself. Sometimes he laughed, and other times he would yell and curse. Although they were just downstairs, his family didn't pay any attention to him. Several times, he knocked on my door asking for water because his mom wouldn't give him any. I gave him water, but drew the line at his request to use my phone.

Mike seemed to be getting worse every day and began to look almost inhuman. I was not afraid of him, but his ranting and raving was becoming a little annoying. A foreboding feeling came over me that something was about to happen. Mike couldn't go on like that much longer without some sort of incident occurring.

My senses were correct and I was awakened early one morning to the sound of a loud bang, then a scream, then yelling. I called the police and the operator informed me that there had already been another call and the police were on their way. As soon as I made my way to the window, four cop cars pulled up. Several of them surrounded the building with their rifles cocked. I yelled to Christine, who can sleep through anything, that there were police with guns outside our apartment. I opened the window in order to eavesdrop. Yes, I am a nosy neighbor, but you would be too if your house was surrounded by the police. Virginia was on the balcony, smoking and talking to the officers who were standing just below her. She informed them that the perpetrator was her son, Mike, and that he had jumped off the balcony and ran down the street before the police arrived. I overheard Virginia telling the cops that her son was schizophrenic and refused to take his medication. Since returning home from jail, Mike had been using crack instead of taking anti-psychotics.

The police took off, hopefully to find the runaway man who should be arrested for waking me up at six o'clock in the morning. I went to work and told everybody in my office about the fiasco. It made for a good story.

The very next day, I had to spend my coveted Saturday morning doing laundry. I threw on whatever clean clothes I could find, grabbed my laundry basket, and opened the front door. As I was about to take a step outside, I had to stop myself in mid-motion and abruptly shut the door. I set my basket on the ground and took a deep breath. Slowly and quietly I opened the door wide enough to squeeze my head outside and make sure my eyes hadn't deceived me. I glanced down, and sure enough, my vision had been correct. Mike was fast asleep in front of my door, with his head resting on the doormat. I shut the door again and paced back and forth in my apartment trying to figure out what to do. I decided I must call the police. After dialing the Hollywood Police Department, a lady came on the line to direct my call. I didn't quite know what to say. "Um, yes. Uhh, well, yesterday the police were looking for a man who escaped and I think he is sleeping on my door step." The operator informed me that she would send someone to come and check it out.

I was trapped in my apartment for an hour and a half before the police came. Again, I woke Christine up to tell her that Mike was camped out in front of our door. We went over to the door and I cracked it open enough for Christine to see that I was not making this up. Unimpressed, she crawled back in bed. Finally, there was a loud pounding on the door. Was it Mike wanting a glass of water and a phone call or was that the police? I nervously went to the door and opened it just enough to see the uniforms and shiny badges of the L.A.P.D. I felt safe and opened the door all the way. The police were undisturbed by Mike, who lay under their feet, and Mike was undisturbed by them, fast asleep. The police looked at me with squinted eyes, as if the situation needed some sort of explanation. I felt it was pretty obvious why I had called them, but they seemed to want me to verbalize that there was an uninvited man sleeping in front of my doorstep.

One of the policemen yelled at Mike to get up. Mike didn't move. The policeman repeated, "Get up, you can't sleep here." And this time he took his foot, gently placed it on Mike's side and nudged him back and forth. Groggy, Mike yawned, rolled over and groaned. The police got Mike to his feet without using too much force. I was under the impression that they were going to arrest him, but they didn't. The police escorted Mike down the stairs. One of the officers yelled back up to me that Mike wouldn't be giving me any more problems.

"We'll see about that," was Mike's response. And with that, the police took off and left me there in the midst of the threat. Now I was pissed. The police took their sweet time getting to my apartment, and then when a convicted felon threatened me, they left me there to deal with it. Whatever happened to serving and protecting? I honestly was not afraid of Mike and didn't really think that he would hurt me. I was angry with the police and their lack of tact, promptness, and concern.

The rest of my day went on as planned. That afternoon, I called my parents to tell them what happened. Actually, I gave them a watered down version to keep them from worrying too much. I left out the part about Mike threatening me, as well as details about his mental instability. Even so, my dad went right out and bought me my first bottle of mace. I suspect that if I had told him the whole story, he might have purchased a trendy little handgun for my purse. I carried the mace around on my key chain for a couple of days and decided it was best to keep it in the junk drawer in my kitchen. The mace was very bulky and I knew that I was more apt to accidentally use it on myself than to ward off predators.

The weekend ended in relative peace. The air was filled with the general day to day noise of the neighborhood, which was peace enough for me. Nobody had been sprayed in the eye and blinded and the space in front of my door was now vacant. It seemed as though life was getting back to normal. I should have known the best was yet to come.

Mike showed up at our front door a few days later. I opened the door to go to work, and there he was, fast asleep with his head resting on the two-dollar Ikea doormat. Because I was running late, there wasn't time to deal with it, so I stepped over him and went on my way. Mike was still sleeping when I came back home; only he had moved the mat and flipped around so that his feet were now in front of the door. I didn't know what to do, so I let him be.

Mike had been living in front of my apartment for over a week before I admitted to myself that he might never leave. Rarely did I find him awake. I have never seen such a champion sleeper. Wrapped from head to toe in a blanket that I assumed had been given to him by his mother, he looked quite cozy on his bed of concrete.

The previous Sunday, I met a guy at church named Chris who was interested in volunteering at HUP. He called me up and wondered if I could give him a tour and tell him about the organization. Forgetting about sleeping beauty, I told him to meet me at my apartment and we could walk over to the community house together. This poor suburban boy knocked on the door so softly I could barely hear it. Chris began to whisper when I opened the door. He stepped inside and I told him he didn't need to whisper. "I didn't want to wake up your roommate," he replied. Startled, I crossed my eyes and looked back at him. When I realized that Chris actually thought that Mike was my roommate and not a stranger sleeping on the porch, I wanted to crack up laughing. Did he think I was the type of person who would allow my roommate to sleep outside? I tried my best not to be condescending when I informed him that the man in question was the schizophrenic, crack addict son of my neighbor. Who else would he be?

When Christine came home, I told her what Chris had said. I warned her not to make me mad or she would have to sleep outside.

It was time to shut down the motel. I didn't want Mike to think he could spend the rest of his years asleep at my doorstep. I came home from work one day and said, "Mike, you need to go now." He didn't move. I shook him a little and said, "I'm serious, you can't stay here anymore." In a sleepy voice, he said he would just sleep a little longer and then he would leave. And stupid me, I believed him.

Several days later, I tried again. I nudged Mike awake and made it clear that he needed to leave immediately. He got up, grabbed his blanket and shuffled away without an argument. And stupid me, I thought that was the end of him.

The next morning, I stepped outside and felt something move

under my foot. I looked down to see Mike, wrapped in the familiar tan blanket with holes. All I could see of him was the top of his curly head. The thought occurred to me that I should have been conditioned to look down before exiting my apartment by now.

I caught a glimpse of a new addition to his temporary home, and his amusing new set up made it clear that he was determined to stay. Writing about it and remembering it now brings a smile to my face. Mike had gathered some of his prize possessions and lined them along the wall of the apartment across from mine. His head was next to the wall opposite my apartment and his feet spread down to my front door. Right next to him, he had placed some items that he must have found difficult living without for so long. The first necessity lined up in order was a large, purple, stuffed animal Barney. Next to Barney was a jar of Goober, that genius concoction of half jelly, half peanut butter in one jar. The next item in line was a stack of about 20 magazines entitled, JuGGs. I will never be able to look at Barney the same way. I think that he was peering down at the magazines, trying to get a peek. Finally, the list of treasures rounded out with some CD's. I went back inside to make Christine take a look. We had a good laugh and went off to work.

My attempts at getting Mike to leave had been futile. It was time to call the police again. I actually felt bad about it, but not bad enough to let Mike keep living outside my door. The police came and helped him gather up his stuff, accusing him of stealing the CD's. They made it clear that he was not to return or he would be arrested. I doubted that this was really the end of him. To be honest, I was even a little sad that it might be.

But Mike never returned to my porch or to the apartment building. I have never seen him again. Sometimes, I wonder about him, what he is doing and whose porch he is sleeping on. I look back with fondness more than anything else, even though the situation was irritating at the time.

Charlie's Angel

One Sunday night after a community dinner at my friend Nancy's apartment, some of us decided to rent a movie. Rob, Christine, and Alastair stayed behind while Catherine, Nancy and I went to Blockbuster video.

We wandered up and down the aisles and none of the movies looked good. It's amazing how that happens in video stores. There are thousands of movies to choose from, but one of two things always happens. Either, you have seen the movie when it was in the theaters, or it looks like total crap and not worth the time or money.

The three of us ended up standing in front of an entire wall dedicated to the movie, *Charlie's Angles*. I quickly announced that the movie looked stupid. The previews indicated that the main objective of the movie seemed to be getting as many butt shots as possible of Lucy Liu, Cameron Diaz, and Drew Barrymore. As I was making my case for not renting this movie, Nancy was giving me a weird look and glancing over my shoulder. I said, "What?" Again she looked over my shoulder and gave me that glare. I couldn't understand what the big deal was until I turned around to see for my myself why she cared so much that I was bashing *Charlie's Angels*. And then, I wanted to remove my foot from my mouth and use it to run out of the store. Not two feet away from me stood Cameron Diaz. I was afraid she might pull out some of her ass-kicking kung fu moves that I had seen in the previews.

Mercifully, Catherine chose a movie and shuffled us into the line. Cameron followed behind us with her selection. I kept peering over at her, partly to see if she was glaring at me and partly because I was curious which movie she was renting. If she had heard my comment, she was very gracious and was not giving me the evil eye. I didn't get to see her choice of movies, but I was relieved to make it out of there without having to use self-defense.

The three of us piled into the car and cracked up. We laughed at the odds that somebody's movie that I was making fun of was standing right behind me. Only in Hollywood. We laughed, too, at the fact that Rob was lazy and stayed behind instead of going to pick out the movie with us. We knew that he was going to be really jealous.

We got home and bragged about our star sighting and Rob was so mad that he almost boycotted staying for the movie. To this day, I don't think that he has ever gotten over missing an encounter with Cameron Diaz. Whenever we tell the story, his demeanor changes and he growls under his breath.

The Unicorn

During a stint of unemployment, I spent a lot of time at the YMCA playing pick up basketball and admiring the attractive men. One day in mid October, my eyes were drawn to one guy in particular, and not because of his jump shot. He was gorgeous with his perfectly sculpted biceps and tattoos on both arms. He looked like the type of guy who dated Victoria's Secret models.

Weeks after I had spied my new favorite basketball player, everything changed. I came into the gym and signed my name on the white board to get on the list to play. A few people were warming up their shots, waiting for that tenth person to roll out of bed and into the Y. I sat at half court, stretching my stiff legs that weren't quite ready to be up and about. Something caused me to lift my eyes and glance toward the door of the gym. My heart raced and then pounded. This was strange since I hadn't started running up and down the court yet. My handsome new crush had entered the gym. Actually, I hadn't even bothered developing a crush on him. There are some people who are too much of a stretch to even dream about. That wasn't going to stop me from admiring his beauty, believe me.

I quickly looked back down at the floor, not wanting to be obvious or seem like I had noticed him. Usually, this keeps men from approaching me, but I could feel him coming towards me. Not only did he head in my direction, he sat down only feet from me. Stay calm. I looked up, smiled and said hi. And then, the miracle happened. Not only did he say hi back, he began a conversation.

"I'm Jesse, what's your name?"

"Mandy," I replied, trying not to sound shocked that he was actually speaking to me.

"Where are you from?" He must have been impressed by my first answer and wanted to know more.

"I'm from San Diego," I announced.

He continued, "What brought you to L.A.?" And there it came; the question that sent people running or brought about an awkward silence.

"I moved here to be a missionary."

"Like with the church?" asked Jesse.

I nodded yes, affirming that I was not a Victoria's Secret model.

Jesse looked at me wide eyed and said; "I didn't know people go to church anymore. You actually go to church? You want to go to church?" Most people typically respond to the fact that I came to Hollywood to be a missionary by quickly changing the subject. I wasn't used to all the questions. But Jesse was actually intrigued and wanted to know more, about me.

"I do go to church on purpose," I said.

That was one of the best basketball games ever. I tried really hard to keep my eye on the ball and focus. Good luck. Praise be to God that Jesse ended up on the skins team. The good Lord was blessing me for talking about church.

Well, you know I couldn't wait to get myself to the gym the next morning for a game of hoops. I stood in front of my dresser digging through t-shirts and gym shorts. I chose the most flattering and laced my tennis shoes. I actually brushed my hair before throwing it into a ponytail. I looked in the mirror, unimpressed. Sexy I was not. What is a girl to do? I can't play basketball in a skirt and I refuse to be one of those girls who cakes on makeup to go to the gym.

I walked into the gym and there was already a game in progress. I eyed the sweaty men running up and down the court. No Jesse. A wave of disappointment swept through me. I took a few steps into the gym, and in an instant, my whole day looked brighter. There he was! Perfect as he removed his shoes, beads of sweat tracing his forehead and falling to the painted lines of the court. I made my way over and sat right next to him. I was not about to waste any more time away from his side. And heart of hearts, joy of joys, he said, "Hello Amanda." Amanda, like he'd known me and loved me from birth. I tried not to sound sad as I asked him if he was done playing. He said that he had played enough basketball for the day. I cursed my need for that extra hour of beauty sleep. My enthusiasm for a game of pick-up quickly waned.

But what came next, I couldn't have orchestrated in my perfect fantasy. We continued talking as we sat on the hardwood floor. Jesse leaned over and asked if I would like to get together for coffee sometime. I politely accepted in a voice that combined excitement and terror. He took out a little piece of paper from his backpack and wrote, Mandy, and in parenthesis, gym rat, with my phone number underneath. I said a quick prayer for that little piece of paper as he slid it into the outer pocket of his backpack. Please, God, protect that paper from unwanted spills or gusts of wind that might sweep it away.

We decided on a lunch date for the next day. I watched him leave the gym and my eyes followed him down the hall. Every inch of me wanted to jump up and do the 'I have a date' dance. Instead, I stood up calmly and added my name to the white board, as if hot men asked me out all the time.

The next morning, I couldn't contain myself. I showered and primped. My long hair was blow dried straight for the first time in months. I carefully applied some makeup and even put on perfume. Once I deemed myself acceptable, I looked over at the clock and found that I still had two hours to kill. I marched down the street to my friends' apartment and announced the good news. I have a date. Though I live in a community of incredibly amazing women, dating is rare. For us, having a date is right up there with winning the lottery. After an hour of soaking up support and encouragement, I headed back home. I checked myself again in the mirror, grateful to be able to wear something other than gym clothes.

 I plopped myself down in my big recliner, a donated item from a nice church couple. I reassured myself that he really was coming. This wasn't just a big, cruel joke. He wasn't going to pretend to want to go out with me and then leave me wondering what happened. This wasn't high school and adults don't do that kind of stuff, do they? Mercifully, there was a knock at the door and I didn't have to play out my worst nightmare in my head any longer.

 As I walked to the door after waiting a few seconds so as not to seem eager, panic and excitement collided in my stomach. I opened the door and there he was. He said "Hi" and I said "Hi" and we just stood there looking at each other, giggling like little kids. I grabbed my sweater and clutched it like a security blanket as we walked to his truck.

 Jesse took me to a Brazilian restaurant on Sunset. My dating experience since college had been limited, and I was so nervous that I had a hard time eating my sandwich. Jesse ordered salmon and plantains, and kept trying to get me to eat the fried bananas. Plantains were not a dish that I was familiar with, and they did not look particularly appetizing. Jesse thought my reaction to his plantains was funny. He thought *I* was funny. After finally agreeing to take a bite, my expression needed no explanation as I slowly chewed the food. He seemed to think that was about the funniest thing he had ever seen and I was pleased with my production.

 After lunch, Jesse wanted to take me to a café for dessert. My stint at lunch had not deterred him from feeding me more food. Somehow, in the ten-minute ride to the delicatessen, some very important information arose. I don't know how these things came up or how we managed to share it all in such a short time frame. Neither of us expected what we heard from the other on this little commute.

Jesse smokes pot. It is not an everyday event, but he smokes with his friends at parties. I see. This is not a big deal to the world in general, I realize. This would not have fazed me two years ago, but for a girl who has recently found her faith and was seeking to live in this faith after several years off the beaten path, pot smoking was problematic. If this was not enough information for a first date, Jesse admitted that he had not had sex in six months and this was some kind of record for him. Now he was in for the surprise. In response to his six-month drought, all I could do was smile and shake my head. This was not my way of judging him; it was just the irony of it all. Jesse could sense there was something behind my reaction, and he said, "What?" with a curious look. I told him that I had made a decision not to have sex until I was married. It's a good thing that we were at a stoplight; otherwise he might have driven into oncoming traffic. My shock at his revelations was nothing compared to his disbelief over mine. Jesse just looked at me in silence for a few seconds. Finally, he said, "You are like the unicorn. I have heard of it, but I have never seen it."

Thank the lucky stars we arrived safely at the café. While sharing a piece of delicious white cake with whipped frosting, I wondered aloud at what we were getting ourselves into. The differences were so pronounced. Jesse just looked at me again in silence. What does this mean? Why does he keep doing that? I have learned that it's his way of getting me to calm down. Take a breath. Relax. His eyes told me that we didn't need to figure everything out right there. We just needed to finish our piece of cake.

Jesse walked me to the door of my apartment. We reenacted the scene at the beginning of the date where we looked at each other and giggled. I could tell he was contemplating a kiss and was hoping he didn't try it. Thankfully, he said he had a good time and that he would call me. I opened the door and sank into the recliner, reaching for the phone to call my friend Nancy and tell her every little detail.

Later that evening, without Jesse there to give me the look that says, "Get a grip," I started wondering how this could ever work out. He is wild and all of the things that I should not be looking for in a man. But there is something about him that draws me in. I know that you are thinking that it's his handsome face and washboard abs, but it goes beyond physical appearance. He is comfortable, like my recliner. When he laughs at something I have said or done, I feel like the queen of Sheba. It seemed best to try and be friends because I didn't want to give him up.

Jesse called the next day, to my delight, and asked if I wanted to see a movie. "Only if it's rated G," I said. He paused, deciding whether or not I was serious. When he realized that I was kidding, he cracked up and I was queen.

We went to dinner at an Indian restaurant before the movie. Jesse was a much more adventurous eater than I was. Our conversation at dinner was life affirming, comfortable, real. I once had a Bible study teacher who said that good conversation is the best aphrodisiac and he is right. In the middle of dinner, Jesse asked me about high school and what that was like for me. Before I could sensor myself, I blurted out that it had been a very difficult time in my life because I had struggled with depression during my junior and senior years. Once that word, depression, had left my tongue, I tried to give him an out from the subject. "You probably don't want to hear about that," I mumbled. He met my eyes in a stare so powerful, I wanted to look down at my plate of curry, but couldn't.

"Those are exactly the kinds of things I want to know about you," he said. "It's not the same old bull shit." It certainly wasn't. I came clean with all the gory details of my teenage misery.

It wasn't long before I had Jesse laughing again at my inexperience with foreign food. He had ordered a variety of meats and vegetables of all colors and textures for us to share. He would place something red and mushy next to some green bits on his fork and coax me into eating it. As soon as that concoction was down my throat, he had another forkful of chicken with some yellow stuff waving in front of me. We laughed and ate and I could feel the sixteen-year-old girl in me healing with every bite.

Late that night, after we had gone to see a movie, we found ourselves at yet another restaurant called Canters. As if I hadn't had enough culinary adventure, Jesse wanted to eat matzo ball soup. As we sat in our booth, I had my arms crossed in front of me, resting on the table. Jesse leaned across and grabbed my forearms in his strong hands. He looked at me and said, "I'm not sure if we are just supposed to be friends or if I am going to marry you." That's not something I heard every day, or ever.

I can't remember spending a day apart from Jesse for two months after that. We lasted as friends for about a week. Then he kissed me one night in the middle of the street, and that was that.

During those first few weeks of our relationship, Jesse said something that surprised and moved me. "I feel like there has been something missing in my life, and I think it might be church." Jesse opened up about a void that he had been feeling in his life that he had been trying to fill with one-night stands and women. It left him empty and he continued to long for something more. We ended up going to church together on the first Sunday in this new relationship. We went to a study on the book of Luke, which was given by the Bible study teacher I mentioned earlier.

After church, we headed to the Hollywood Farmer's market for lunch, which would become our weekly routine. We stood in line waiting to order tamales, and Jesse held my hand and kissed my cheek right there in front of everybody. I asked him what he thought about church as we sat on the sidewalk and ate our tamales. He hesitated and I could tell he was looking for words that would not disappoint me. Jesse was not ready for church. He wasn't ready for the drastic change it would mean in his life. He said, "I just can't be that good." I tried to explain that God loves him the way he is now and that going to church is an extension of a relationship with a God who knows all of our shortcomings and takes us just as we are. He didn't buy it. Church to him was a bunch of holy people congregating to pat themselves on the back for being good that week and learning how to do it again next week. He is not alone in his view and sometimes I feel the same way.

Jesse was very respectful and supportive of the way I chose to live my life, it just wasn't for him. He was amused when I said shoot instead of shit. (Not that I don't say shit when the situation calls for it). The things that endeared me to him were the things that made us so different. We kept each other entertained as we learned more about each other.

Every year, the Hollywood Urban Project has a Christmas celebration. Some years, we have a posada that reenacts Mary and Joseph's search for shelter. This year, we had a Christmas program at the community house. Jesse accompanied me and met some of my friends for the first time. As we were singing the song about the little drummer boy, Jesse leaned over and whispered, "Are these your unicorn friends?" Pa-rum-pa-pum-pum.

I whispered back that indeed they were.

"Even the guys?"

"As far as I know." I smiled and held his hand, knowing that he was in awe of the possibility.

Well, upon hearing the story of the unicorn, my friends took it and ran with it. To this day, the unicorn is alive and well. My friend, Amy, received a porcelain unicorn as a gift and it has served as a mascot for single women in our neighborhood. Stacey was the first to get married, and then Amy. The unicorn gets passed to the next in line. Kari is engaged and is in possession of the unicorn. If Jesse only knew what he started.

I want to spend some time talking about the unicorn status. Growing up in the church, it was apparent that premarital sex was right up there with murder and stealing. My Bible doesn't have Moses bringing this commandment down from Mount Sinai, but it seems that some people's do. I grew to fear sex as something evil. Along with being afraid of the act of sex, it seemed that talking about it was also taboo.

In college, I spent two and a half years of my life hiding from God and the faith I had once professed. I wanted to try new things and experience the world. I felt I had to deny my relationship with God in order to drink and party and date because I would be a hypocrite otherwise. I found that those things did not fill me like my relationship with God once had. The more I partied, the emptier I felt. During my senior year of college, I came back to my faith and gave my life back to God. I came to view alcohol as the root of evil and saw men as the enemy. I had abused both, and I didn't know how to live a faithful life without being legalistic.

I hadn't dated in two years before I met Jesse. I seemed to think that I would meet a nice Christian boy at church, we would date for the appropriate amount of time, get married and have sex. I didn't meet any nice Christian boys at church that I found appealing or who showed the slightest bit of interest in me. Things weren't working out as planned. Nonetheless, I was the epitome of holiness and pleasing to God because I was not wasting my time with men. This is what I thought.

Even though Jesse never tried to force me to change my mind about this whole unicorn thing, my attraction to him made it very difficult. I wrestled with the fact that I was a twenty-four year old woman who should be able to do what she pleased, and the conviction that I had deep in my heart. I learned in high school youth group to wait until marriage to have sex. This is pleasing to God. This is the best way. But then, I grew up and the church was silent on the issue. What about single people in their 20's and 30's? Silence. What about people who have been divorced? Silence. The church has failed to address the issue but continues to make it known that sex outside of marriage is sin.

Jesse and I broke up over sex. At the time, it was the right decision, though it was sad and painful. Three years have passed and I don't have any regrets. Jesse opened my eyes to spiritual issues that I was not aware of. He was kind and generous and helped me heal in areas of my life that were open wounds. I am grateful to him and treasure the time we spent together.

As time has passed, I know now that God is much more gracious than I had given him credit for. My faith is not about what I do or don't do. It is about my own personal relationship with God. I can't do anything to make him love me less and I can't win more love by being a unicorn.

Depression

Depression. The word alone sounds bleak. Depression and I are well acquainted. We go way back. It has come into my life uninvited on several occasions and made its imprint on my soul. My depression is hard to put into words, but I will do my best to help you enter into the darkness that has invaded my world for many periods in my life.

My most recent episode began after I lost my job in September of 2001. It came upon me gradually and I kept thinking that it would go away and bother someone else. It didn't go away and began pestering me more intensely. At the time, I was dating Jesse, and this caused me to be in denial about the depression. In the past when I was depressed, I imagined that everything would be okay if I were just in a relationship with somebody I really cared about and who would support me. I was confused because Jesse was extremely supportive and I should have been happy. Then I started to imagine that everything would be okay if I just had a job. That was the detail that would solve my discontent. I tend to live like this far too often, even when I am not depressed. I think to myself that I will be content when

I have this or that, but then when I get this or that, I decide that I will really be content when I get something else entirely. Somehow, it is never enough and I realize after a few cycles that this is a bad game without an end.

The beginning stages of the depression looked like apathy. I would have a lunch date with Jesse and not be excited. It wasn't because of anything to do with Jesse, but I had a hard time being interested in anything. I would look through my closet and think that I should wear something cute and feminine, but decisions were hard to make and sweats were the most appealing option.

Fatigue plagued me and I was unable to concentrate. I often had a difficult time focusing in conversations and keeping track of what was said. It is similar to when you are driving and space out and come to realize that you have gone several miles with no recollection of how you came as far as you did.

Thankfully, I had a wonderful therapist named Sue. I had been with her for quite a while because she was the same person who led our group therapy my city dweller year. I had been seeing her individually for about a year and she knew my history well. Sue was able to tie together the effects of experiences and relationships from my past with my current struggles. I used to want to hang an 8x10 photograph of Sue on my mantle, surrounded by flowers and candles to pay homage to her. During the week, I would count down the days until I went to see her. She helped me to have hope and believe that I would get better. I could feel that she really wanted me to be able to live in joy and I came to want that for myself as well, just so that I could please her.

After Jesse and I broke up, I rapidly declined and I could not function much of the time. Days drifted by and I had no memory of having done anything with the time. Every day was a struggle to feel alive. Even sadness would have been welcome because the overwhelming emptiness dulled me to the point where I no longer felt human. I was like a rock or a plastic doll, motionless, expressionless, tossed aside to be trampled on or placed on a shelf in a dark corner of a teenage girls room. I passed hours lying on the floor of my bedroom, unable to get up. I forgot what it was like to care or have energy or feel anything beyond despair. I was in a blur; a deep fog that kept me from seeing past the moment. Depression is a form of death. Your pulse still beats as normal, but your soul is halfway to hell.

I kept a fifth of vodka hidden under my bed. This helped me during the times that I needed to leave the apartment, but didn't have the energy or motivation to get up. My friend Nancy was very patient with me and tried to get me to go places with her. I knew that I needed to get out even if I didn't feel like it, so I would take some swigs of vodka while she was on her way to pick me up.

The depression caused me to struggle spiritually. Prayer felt like an impossible effort. God seemed distant even though my faith told me he was right by my side. I remembered the scripture verse that said He would never leave me or forsake me, but that felt like a big lie. I wanted to yell at God, but I didn't have the energy. I wanted to beg Him for mercy and patience, but I couldn't find words. My eyes couldn't focus on the pages of my Bible. Even so, I was able to express myself through the lyrics of a song entitled *At the Moment* by the band, Stavesacre. This song was my prayer when I could not pray. I needed this prayer to keep living each day and cling to the hope that there was a purpose to my life. The chorus reads:

> My soul will wait
> My soul wait silently
> For God my God
> And I will live
> And know some destiny still waits for me

I listened to this song at least once a day. It was the only time I was able to cry. It still brings tears to my eyes and reminds me of how far I have come.

Another person I relied on during this difficult time was my mom, whom I called several times a day. This was an interesting choice, because my mom didn't understand depression. She grew up on a farm where hard work was of high value and depression would have been seen as laziness. Depression can be very difficult to understand for those who have not experienced it. The fact that I was having such a hard time functioning didn't make sense to my mom. If I had been homeless, or starving, or stricken with a serious illness, then depression would have been warranted. But there really wasn't anything to be depressed about. That is one of the worst things about depression. It can be very isolating because people who have not gone through it often see depression as a choice, when it feels more like a terminal illness.

My mom did her best to understand me, and I leaned on her. I would call her from the floor of my room and inform her that I could not get up. My mom's response: "Go bake some cookies." We would argue for a bit about her not understanding me and being completely ignorant about my suffering. After that didn't work, I would tell her that I didn't have any eggs so that she would get off the cookies. But then she would tell me to go buy some eggs, as if that was the easiest thing in the world to do. I would remind her once again that I couldn't get off the floor, but she wouldn't let me off the hook. She just kept on with those damn eggs and chocolate chip cookies.

After hanging up, I would lie there and contemplate getting up. I would count to three. Nothing. I'll get up in five more minutes. Nothing. It would eventually take me about an hour and some vodka to push myself up and plant my feet on the ground. Okay, I was up. Now, I had to get one whole block to the Sav On. I dragged myself down the street and located the eggs in the refrigerator section. After paying the cashier and doing my best to appear sane, I dragged myself back again with my purchase and baked some fine chocolate chip cookies. Surprisingly, the baking would help me feel better. Not better enough to become a productive member of society, but a little less miserable.

Looking back, I am so grateful to my mom for hanging in with me. I would not have been able to function as much as I did if she hadn't been coaxing me to get out of my apartment daily. Instead of allowing me to wallow in my own self-pity, which I became very good at doing, she helped me do those small, daily activities that felt impossible.

The cookies I had baked were set-aside for Christine. I didn't dare eat them because along with the depression, I had a nice bout of bulimia. I had struggled with eating disorders of various types since high school. In fact, I can remember the exact day that my battle with food and dieting began. I was in the ninth grade and had been playing basketball after school. Once practice was over, my dad was going to drop me off at a friend's house for a slumber party. On the way to the party, we stopped by Denny's restaurant. I didn't even bother looking at the menu because I wasn't hungry. I ordered a glass of lemonade, no big deal. My dad dropped me off at my friend's house and we had a fun night of gossiping and talking about boys.

The next morning, there were several boxes of donuts set out for breakfast. Some of the girls didn't want any breakfast. They said they weren't hungry in that donuts are fattening tone of voice. I started wondering if I should eat one or not. Definitely not, I decided. But they looked so good with their sprinkles and glaze. Maybe I do need to drop a few pounds, though. I went back and forth about whether or not to eat one stupid donut, weighing the pros and cons as if it were an important life decision. I ended up eating two donuts. It was the first time in my life that I felt guilty for eating food when it was breakfast time and I was hungry. That morning, I became aware of dieting and body image. I learned that skinny is good and fat is bad, a lesson that the other girls had apparently already been taught. This was the beginning point of a struggle that has caused me to waste so much precious time agonizing about food and my body.

I look back at the girl sitting across from her father at Denny's and long to go back to her innocence. She didn't even consider calories or fat content. She knew she wasn't hungry, and let that lead her.

After that day, menus became my archenemy. I would examine them intently, identifying the least fattening possibilities. A battle would begin in my mind over whether or not to order what I really wanted, the cheeseburger, or what I should eat, the salad. It was torture for me. The waitress would come to the table and I would order the salad, dressing on the side please. The drink was a no brainer. I always ordered water or diet coke. Regular soda or juice didn't even tempt me anymore. I wasn't about to waste calories on a drink.

At night, when I was lying in bed, I would add up the amount of calories I had eaten during the day over and over in my head. I began taking diet pills and examining my stomach in the mirror, disgusted by what I saw. Thoughts of food became an obsession and I was more proud of myself when I passed up eating a cookie than when I did well on a test.

Needless to say, I had low self-esteem in high school. I thought that I was fat and ugly and I hated myself. My first bout of depression began my junior year and lasted almost two years. The depression looked different than my most recent episode, however. I was able to function and go to school and play basketball. I wasn't in a fog, but I was extremely sad all the time. I used to walk down the halls of my high school and pray for God to help me and be with me. I cried in my room after school every day for no apparent reason. I fantasized about what it would be like to run my car off the freeway and die. My journals contained different versions of suicide notes and I enjoyed fantasizing about what my funeral would be like. People at school who never paid attention to me might feel guilty or sad for having looked right through me. For once, I would be the center of attention. Even though I thought about killing myself, I just couldn't go through with it. I sort of resigned myself to the belief that this was my lot in life. The idea that I would ever feel okay seemed impossible, and I really thought that I was going to spend the rest of my life in sadness, hating myself.

Part of what was so hard about the situation was not having any idea what was wrong with me. Nobody ever talked about depression and it wasn't a word that I knew to connect with my experience. I felt so ashamed to hate myself the way that I did, so I didn't tell anybody.

I even had a therapist that I saw for a year and I never once told her how much pain I was in. My parents became very concerned, but I couldn't share my struggles with them because I didn't know how to verbalize my emotions. I had all of these horrible feelings that banged around in my brain without being able to escape through my mouth.

School was a daily battle to appear as sure of myself as possible, while inside I was all mixed up and full of sorrow. There are two high school memories in particular that remain vivid images of the person I was, or at least, the person that my peers thought me to be. I always wonder if the popular people harbor ill thoughts about high school or if their thoughts drift to parties where they were the center of attention, football games where they made the winning touch down, or school dances where they had the most coveted date. I will just inform you up front, as if you could not have already guessed, that these were not among my memories. I was the girl who tried hard to look like she didn't care. My school had a strict dress code, complete with a uniform of saddle shoes and a plaid, pleated skirt. It was difficult to find a way of being unique and rebelling through fashion, but I did my best. It was popular for the girls to roll their skirts at the waste, shortening the hemline to just below the butt. In addition to wearing my skirt right at the knee, I brushed my hair about twice a week and boycotted make up almost entirely. I felt like crap, so I thought I might as well look like it too. I wasn't one of those kids that got tortured or harassed. I was on friendly-ish terms with everybody, without being connected to a close-knit group of friends. I felt like I might as well have been invisible.

Well, one day during a free period, I was sitting on the senior bench with a few other people. Peter and Desiree were discussing various movies that were popular at the time. I didn't talk much, as was my habit, so my role in the conversation was basically to nod in approval of whoever looked at me for support. Desiree started in on a monologue about the wonders of the movie, *Reality Bites*. I really had wanted to see this movie and was interested in their reviews, so I opened my mouth and asked some questions. Peter looked over at me and smiled in a condescending way. I felt the sting before any words even left his mouth. "You wouldn't like that movie," he said. "It's a chick movie." I am so proud of myself that I did not cry or run off or punch his lights out. I sat in silence during the rest of the period and opted not to inform Peter of the obvious, that I am, indeed, a chick.

The next wonderful memory was captured in the yearbook, so God forbid I should forget; a reminder is bound up for all time. I was voted, drum roll please, most likely to be seen lifting weights. Now you aren't feeling like Peter is such an ass, are you? Yes, that's right, every senior girl dreams of receiving this accolade, but back off girls, it's mine. I feel I must explain this title, and I wish they had written a little side bar into the yearbook as well. Basketball was one of the only things that kept me from slitting my wrists in high school. I loved it and I was good at it. My dream was to get a scholarship to play in college and my hopes may have been shattered when I tore ligaments in my knee my junior year. In order to come back from this injury, I worked extremely hard to build up the muscles in my legs. Thus, I spent time in the weight room with all the jocks, pumping iron and getting strong. I don't remember ever seeing another girl lifting weights, so I pretty much steam rolled the competition in this yearbook category. I'm sure I probably had a few votes for the most likely to succeed and the prettiest smile, but they couldn't give me all of the awards, now could they?

When I left high school and moved to Indiana for college, I met some incredible people that came into my life and helped me move from sadness to joy. My friends and extended family in Indiana loved me, and in turn, I learned to love myself. I am so grateful for that time in my life, where I learned about the importance of having female friends to talk to about problems and life. My new girlfriends loved Taco Bell and sweets and never talked about calories. I began to learn how to enjoy food without obsessing about it or worrying about getting fat.

Somehow, during my third year in Los Angeles, all of my insecurities about body image and weight began to take over. I started examining my body and finding flaws that needed to be fixed with diet and exercise. At the time, it seemed like a good idea to eat a bunch of food and then throw it up. I wanted to lose some weight because it was summer time and my bikini was calling to me from its storage place. I didn't want to give up eating delicious food, so I thought that this was the perfect solution.

After a few months of throwing up my food, I decided that it probably wasn't such a good plan. Plus, I had heard that bulimia causes your teeth to turn yellow and that is just as unattractive as cellulite.

By October, I had begun dating Jesse and this helped the situation incredibly. He liked to eat and was always trying to feed me. I didn't worry about my weight because I knew that Jesse liked me for who I was. I felt like I could put on thirty pounds and he wouldn't care, even if I would have been mortified.

After the break up, the problem reared its ugly head again. This time, I was unable to control it. I would become overwhelmed by anxiety, and it wouldn't subside unless I went to the bathroom and threw up my food. I got really scared because I no longer had control over myself when I would feel the need to purge. Finally, I let Sue in on the problem. We had been focusing on the depression, and frankly, I wasn't ready to give up my obsession with weight and food. I thought that getting better meant getting fatter.

Sue helped me come up with a plan. When I felt the overwhelming urge to make myself throw up, I was to call a friend, go shopping, or somehow distract myself. The problem was that I was still depressed and had a hard time being proactive about anything. After eating, I ended up gluing myself to the recliner in my living room until the anxiety passed. I lost track of time in that chair and just sat and sat as long as I needed to.

During this time, a friend of mine admitted that he was an alcoholic and began attending A.A. meetings. I decided to go with him to show my support and encouragement. When I went to my first A.A. meeting, I didn't have any idea how much I needed to be surrounded by people who were openly dealing with their problems.

I felt like I had come home to a place that was familiar and free. For once, I didn't have to pretend that I was okay. In the midst of this group of strangers, I finally had a sense of being known for who I truly was and being accepted as such. All of the ways in which I tried to mask my misery from the outside world were not necessary during the two-hour meeting. I could breath. I could feel like I wasn't the only messed up person on the planet who was self-destructive. I began to open myself up to the possibility of getting better.

Thankfully, it didn't take me long until I was healed from bulimia and praise be to God that it has not come back since. With the help of my therapist, I realized that the disease is not about food, but rather control. I had lost control of so many things in my life, and so I attempted to control food. Even now, when I start thinking about body image and wishing I looked better, I can see that what I am really doing is grasping for control. Recently, I got a tattoo of birds flying up my side to symbolize freedom from the grip that the eating disorder had over my life. I felt like I had been caged in, unable to move without banging up against the walls that kept me trapped. Once I began to accept and even love my body, I was able to fly out of the confines of my own self-hatred and truly live in freedom.

While I won the battle over bulimia, I was still struggling against depression. I ended up getting back the job that I had lost in September, which helped quite a bit. The depression became less debilitating and I was able to get to work every day. I was still in a daze and had a hard time focusing, but at least I wasn't lying on the floor or sipping vodka at noon.

I worked as a bilingual coordinator at an elementary school. During that time, there were a few sources of joy that spread some light into my dark world. One of these rays of light was my community. The other was a third grade class at school.

My friend, Stacey, who was a city dweller the year before me and part of my community, was the teacher of this light-bearing group of third graders. It was a small class of twelve students, but the room was full of personality.

Every Friday was fun Friday. If the students turned in all of their homework for the week, they got to bring their lunch back to the classroom on Friday instead of eating outside at the tables. Fun Friday consisted of eating inside and radio Disney. You might be thinking to yourself that fun Friday doesn't sound very exciting. Well, you would be wrong. The classroom became Studio 54, or at least the elementary school version, and Stacey and I got free entertainment. Julia was little miss Britney Spears in training. She would lead the other girls in dance moves that looked like they came straight from the latest Backstreet Boy, N Sinc, and Christina Aguilera videos. Julia is going to be trouble come junior high. Efraim could break dance, which sent all the girls into a tizzy, including Stacey and me. We would beg him to do it and he would wait until the proper amount of attention was focused on him. We would go wild after he spun around on the floor, flipping his body around in an amazing fashion. Efraim would stand up and simply shrug his shoulders as we clapped and cheered. He tried to teach me one time and I ended up looking like one of the fish from the class aquarium had been thrown onto the alphabet rug and was thrashing about.

And then there was my favorite. I know, teachers and people who work with kids aren't supposed to have favorites, but Stacey and I did. Pablo was the kid who was four years away from getting slammed into lockers and de-pantsed in gym class. Thankfully, third graders are still pretty nice and don't harass the chubby kids as much as seventh graders. Pablo was an adorable chunk with never ending cheeks; wire rimmed glasses and an abnormally large head.

Pablo loved fun Fridays. He did not partake in the dancing, but he bestowed upon himself a very important job. Pablo was in charge of writing the name of the artist and the title of the song on the white board. Aaron Carter and Jessica Simpson were listed next to the vocabulary words for the day. Pablo took pride in his job. He wrote neatly and promptly. I never had to think to myself, "I wonder who sings this fine song?" or "What on earth could the title of this catchy tune be?"

Every Friday was hilarious and fun, but there are two Fridays that stand out in particular. They both involve Pablo, of course. The first episode occurred when the majority of the class, Pablo not included, decided to listen to Star 98.7 instead of radio Disney. Pablo was beside himself. He tried to convince his peers to change the station, but they ignored his pleas. Pablo sat down and refused to inform us of the names of the artists. Stacey and I kept peering over at him to make sure he was okay. He seemed to be working on something feverishly at his desk. Minutes later, Pablo was marching around the room, dodging mini Britney and her entourage. He was holding up a pencil with a piece of construction paper taped to the top that said, 'We want radio Disney.' Pablo was on strike. None of the other kids paid him any attention, but Stacey and I were in stitches at the back of the room. Pablo spent the whole lunch hour picketing.

Not long after Pablo went on strike, radio Disney was in full swing and Pablo must have been in a particularly good mood because he abandoned his station at the white board and was standing next to Stacey's desk, lost in the music. It was obvious that he was in his own world, oblivious to the eyes on him. Pablo began to dance. It was not just any dance. He was leaning over the desk, knees bent with his hands out in front of him holding onto the top of the table. His butt was in the air and he was shaking it every which way. When his butt went to the right, his head moved to the left in an upward fashion. When his butt went to the left, his head came back down and swung up again to the right. His movements were calculated and he was feeling the music. It looked like an exotic dance show and I felt like I shouldn't be watching. Pablo must have felt us observing him, because as soon as he thought someone was looking, he went back over to his station at the white board and stood completely still.

Despite the fact that work was going well and I was no longer struggling with bulimia, the depression just wouldn't subside. My therapist and I discussed the possibility of medication. Since I had a history of depression and I had been struggling with it for about six months, Sue thought that I should schedule an appointment with a psychiatrist. I had really wanted to beat this thing on my own, but the idea of popping a few pills and feeling better was very tempting. Sue gave me the name and number of a psychiatrist that she had worked with for years.

I had considered myself to be strong and brave because I could win this fight without the help of anti-depressants. I have since learned from personal experience, books, and classroom lectures, that the combination of medication and therapy provide the best outlook for healing.

I finally gave up on plan A, to heal myself, and opted for plan B, medication. I dialed the number for the psychiatrist and spoke with a receptionist. She gave me the estimates of the three necessary visits, and I immediately liked the sound of plan A again. It would cost over 500 dollars for three visits, not including the medication. If I hadn't been depressed before, I would be after forking over 500 bucks to some shrink.

I spent a week contemplating the two options. I had begun to look forward to getting medication. The idea of feeling better really began to appeal to me. I became discouraged and knew that I wasn't going to be able to fight this battle on my own, as originally planned. I began to rack my brain for a possible solution, when I remembered that many people from my neighborhood who did not have health insurance and couldn't afford medical attention had been referred to the Los Angeles Free Clinic. Perhaps they had a psychiatrist. I grabbed the phone book and dialed the number. A nurse answered who sounded like she had grown tired of taking calls and making appointments all day. I politely and sweetly asked if they had a psychiatrist on staff, with the hope that she would be empathetic and helpful despite her irritating job. The nurse did not make sweet talk back, but she did get me an appointment with the psychiatrist, Dr.

Vick for a month later, and that was good enough for me.

It turned out that Dr. Vick only works at the clinic on Friday evenings, so all of the mental health cases arrive in one group at 7 o'clock and wait their turn for a listening ear and most importantly, a prescription. I sauntered into the clinic at the designated hour, already feeling better at the idea of help. I scribbled my name on the sign in sheet and crawled over several people to get to an empty chair. The waiting room reminded me more of the DMV than a hospital. Suddenly, I got an uncomfortable feeling as I noticed the other people waiting to see Dr. Vick. I cautiously turned my head to get a glimpse of the man sitting to my left. I was drawn to him because he could not stop fidgeting. One foot tapped, while his head clicked ever so slightly. His hands were in a wrestling match and couldn't keep from attacking each other. His eyes were blood shot and his arms were hosts to tract marks. He seemed wild and disheveled, clearly a drug addict. I moved my stare to the man, no woman, no man, sitting on my right. I had climbed over this man to get to my seat and his knees were right up against the chair in front of him. He had on a woman's business suit and dress flats, size thirteen no doubt. His face was home to the largest nose I had ever seen, with warts or zits or craters growing all over it. His long brunette wig looked like a horse's main that must have been purchased at the 99-cent store, where he must have also bought his purse. As a man, he would have been unattractive, but as a woman, he was down right terrifying.

I looked around the rest of the room, stale and shabby with posters about aids and pregnancy prevention. I became aware that I was feeling above these people and this place. A bolt of humility almost struck me to my knees. I had grown up going to Kaiser hospital, where the waiting room has carpet and People magazines, the chairs aren't stained with God knows what, and the people are sick, but normal. But there I was, sitting between an addict and a transvestite, just as poor and hurting as they were. I was in no position to judge or feel myself to be any better than they were. Upon that realization, I wanted to reach out and hold their hands as an apology for my pride and a gesture of solidarity in our struggles. I wanted to weep at my own insensitivity and capacity for cruelty. I had truly thought that I had moved past all my feelings of superiority due to skin color and socioeconomic status after I had lived in the neighborhood for so long. They came right up from wherever they had been hiding and slapped me across the face, challenging me to confront them. It is painful to become aware of the ugly parts of yourself. I like to think of myself as someone who is passionate about social justice and the fight against oppression. It was hard for me to realize that in the war against prejudice and inequality, I was the one who needed to change and be humbled.

I left the clinic that night with a bottle of antidepressants and a dose of conviction. I needed to face the ability that is within me to tear down another person whom I didn't even know. It was time to take a microscope to the dark places I had avoided acknowledging within me, and bring them out in the open where they could be molded and transformed. I have come to realize that this is an ongoing process, never completed, but hopefully always in progress. The minute I feel I have arrived is the time to be worried that pride is seeping in.

After two years of taking my pills every night before bed, I gradually began to lower the dosage under the supervision of Dr. Vick. My mood and emotional state had been very "normal" since the medication had been regulated so long ago.

I have been off the medication for two years, and thankfully, I feel no difference than when I was taking it. I may have another bout of depression in my lifetime, and I am relieved to know that medication works for me. The first time I find myself stuck to the floor for no apparent reason and unable to get up, I am picking up the phone to call my psychiatrist and get me some pretty pink pills.

Do you ever wonder, in the midst of a horrible situation or

experience or life, for that matter, what it's all about and if there is some purpose or meaning behind it? I never did. But people were sure to remind me of the possibility. I couldn't stand it when nice and helpful friends and family members would inform me "something good will come out of this." I wanted to respond by waving my middle finger as I pulled my vodka out from under the bed and poured the entire contents in a plastic cup. I never had the guts to do this, so I smiled and nodded, the way you do in foreign countries where you don't speak the language.

The kicker was that I knew they were probably right, but there was no way I was going to admit it. Well, those annoying people turned out to have hit the nail right on the head, with my fingers holding it up. At first, it hurt to be wrong, but then, I was grateful. Now I can see the ways in which my experiences, as much as they sucked, were leading me to my calling in life. I have recently obtained my degree in marriage and family therapy, which will enable me to help others who have struggled with depression and eating disorders. I don't necessarily want to be a therapist, but now in addition to my own experience, I have training that will help me be a support to others. Okay, okay, good did come out of my suffering after all.

Alberto

Alberto, the youngest member of the HUP volleyball team and brother of my beloved Jessica, was shot and killed in a drive by shooting on Sunday night, August 6th 2001. I came home from work on Monday to hear Melissa's panicked voice on my answering machine, telling me the awful news and asking me to meet her at Jessica's apartment as soon as I got this message. Shock and disbelief flooded through my body as I took off running down the street. I arrived at the apartment to find Jessica surrounded by Melissa and Carla, offering tissues, loving hugs, kind words. Jessica was not crying, her face hard as she clung to the walls that had begun building back up around her heart. She lay stiff in my embrace, arms down at her side. All I could think to do was tell her that I loved her. Jessica's mother, Isabel, came up and slid into my arms as Jessica peeled herself out of my grasp. Isabel buried her face in my chest, reached her arms around my waste and clasped her hands together. At first, she mumbled into my chest, "por que, por que?" (why, why?) The whisper grew louder until she was squeezing my upper arms in her hands, peering up into my face and crying, "Pobresito my hijo. Como voy a vivir sin el? (My poor son. How am I going to live without him?)" I remained silent, praying for wisdom, strength, and guidance, as I looked down at Isabel, unable to respond with a single word. The air around me grew thick and heavy, like a fog had suddenly descended from heaven. My breathing became labored and the lack of air made me dizzy. I leaned my back up against the closet door, still wearing Isabel around my front like an apron.

Isabel wanted to show me the place where Alberto had been killed. She felt close to him, almost as if he were there with her, when she sat in the spot where Alberto took his last breath. Isabel and I walked the two blocks arm in arm, slowly putting one foot in front of the other. At the rate we were going, I thought it would be midnight by the time arrived. Isabel took steps like a toddler new to walking, using my arm to steady herself.

Finally, we reached the apartment building and sat down on the steps. Most of the blood had been cleaned from the stairs, but the stains remained. A memorial for Alberto had been set up around the front of the building, decorated with flowers, candles, pictures, and stuffed animals. RIP 'El Malo' (Bad) was spray-painted along the wall and I learned that Alberto (El Malo) and one of his best friends, Eddy, had joined the gang, TMC, a month earlier. I rested my head on Isabel's shoulder as she cried softly. Guilt was the first emotion that I felt, not sadness. I should have done more to make sure that Alberto didn't feel the need to join a gang. He and Eddy had practically grown up in the community house going to Bible studies, tutoring, volleyball practice, and the after school program. I felt like we had failed him; I had failed him.

And then my guilt turned into anger directed at God. Why did you let this happen? God, where are you? I am sitting here beside a mother who is in agony. Do something, God. Take it back and do yesterday over.

I racked my brain for the appropriate comforting words to share with Isabel. I longed to say something profound or helpful to ease the pain. I have realized since then that the belief that I can do or say anything to remove the suffering is insensitive and self centered.

As Isabel and I were resting against each other, trying to make sense of what had happened and the reality of death, a group of five gang members came up to us. It was obvious who they were from the TMC tattoos on their necks and arms. Four of them stayed back, while a boy of about seventeen made his way up the steps to where we were sitting. The boy reached into his pocket and pulled out a wad of money, handed it to Isabel and told her that more would be on the way. I looked at stack of bills in Isabel's fist and I felt like I was in a Hollywood crime movie, because things like that don't happen in real life, at least not to me. It was blood money, payment to keep her quiet and cooperative. She thanked him and tried to get details about what had happened the previous night. The boy was vague, not wanting to incriminate himself or any of the others, placing the blame on the rival gang. We later learned from neighbors and other witnesses that the other TMC youth who had been present during the shooting, took off running and left Alberto bleeding on the steps alone. When the shooting had stopped, nobody came to Alberto's aid. He was the only one that had been hit, and was killed by a single bullet when a car drove by and started firing on the crowd of teenagers.

TMC immediately began putting pressure on Eddy to get revenge. HUP was able to put together their own wad of money and with the approval of his parents, Dan bought Eddy a plane ticket to Mexico so that he could stay with family. Eddy left the country two days after the shooting and stayed in Mexico for two years before returning to Los Angeles.

The night following Alberto's death, HUP planned a candle light vigil and procession from the community house to the place where Alberto died. A group of youth, concerned parents, and HUP volunteers, gathered outside of the community house to pray before walking to the memorial. Teenage boys', whom I had always known to be tough and macho, broke down before my eyes. My own tears fell quickly now as I grieved for what Alberto's loss meant to me, but also for the pain so vividly before me on the faces of friends and family. Arm in arm, Isabel and I followed the others in a route we were becoming all too familiar with. Jessica was still trying to be strong, not wanting others to see her get emotional.

A few months before Alberto died, he had been sent to boot camp. After Bible study one evening, Carrie took the girls to the Sav On drug store before dropping them off at home. She noticed that Jessica had purchased a card for Alberto and stole a glance at what it said. The outside of the card had a typical scene of a peaceful river, and at the bottom were the words, "The shortest verse in the Bible is sometimes the one we most need to hear." The inside of the card said, "Jesus wept." I wanted Jessica to allow herself the same freedom that she had given her brother.

As our group had gone about half way on our journey, three police cars pulled up in front of our procession and stopped us in our tracks. The officers got out of the cars, rounded up eight of the high school boys, and shoved them spread eagle with their hands on their heads against the cars. Dan tried to explain that they were with us and had done nothing wrong. Children and parents stared in disbelief as these youth were humiliated for no reason. I can't imagine what it was like for them to be mourning the death of a friend, on their way to pay tribute, and arrested for having brown skin and wearing baggy pants. Racial profiling is alive and well, used by law enforcement to monitor people who look suspicious merely because of their appearance. I used to think that the police were fair and helpful, serving society and protecting us from harm. I didn't understand why they were called pigs and hated by so many people. But I am white and a woman at that, so I have never been arrested for walking down the street, minding my own business.

The cops finally let the boys go and we continued on our way. I tried to console some of them, but they were so mad and embarrassed that they didn't want to follow the group. I imagine that it would be difficult to want to be good and obey the law, when you get searched and questioned even if you aren't doing anything wrong.

I didn't know quite what to expect during the vigil, so I was not prepared for the emotional roller coaster that was about to ensue.

Isabel, Jessica, and her aunt sat down on the cement before the make shift shrine. Jessica could not keep her sadness bottled up any longer and began to cry, asking over and over, "why did he have to die?" Isabel and her sister both began sobbing, then screaming. Agony spread across their faces as they rocked back and forth. I had never seen grief take this form, and it scared me. I stepped back and listened as their cries pierced the night sky and lifted to heaven, praying that God would send comfort or peace or anything to stop the spectacle that I was witnessing. But the yelling carried on well into the evening and those who had gathered to mourn became spectators in a wrestling match between a mother and God. This was grief in its purest form, open wide and uncensored. The aftermath of death that I had experienced previously did not resemble this physical outpouring of sorrow. I envisioned people sitting in church, dabbing at the corners of eyes with a tissue, and politely blowing noses.

I longed to be of help, to comfort or serve, but I was paralyzed by fear as I observed the most horrible ordeal possible; a mother grieving for her dead child. A voice inside my head kept saying, "do something," but I remained at the back of the group at a loss for words or actions that might be of some assistance. As it turns out, Melissa and Carla knew exactly what to do, lovingly and naturally caring for the grieving women. Melissa knelt behind Isabel and Carla was by the side of the aunt. I watched in awe as these two teenage girls tenderly rubbed the backs of the grieving women and wiped their tears away with the sleeves of their sweaters, providing physical comfort and allowing them to mourn. It was a strangely beautiful sight and I felt so proud of the girls for doing what the adults standing by could not do.

Even with the support and assistance of Melissa and Carla, the exhaustion of grief became too much for Isabel to bear. Thankfully, the high school boys drove up and were coming to rejoin our group. They helped Isabel into their car and drove her back home. The girls and I followed on foot and our group of mourners disbanded.

When I arrived at the apartment, Isabel was in a trance like state. I tried to help her take off her shoes so that she could go to bed. She refused to sleep because she thought that someone was going to call and say that Alberto was alive and she could go pick him up. If Isabel allowed herself to sleep, it meant that she had given in to the permanence of death. I sat helplessly on the couch as Isabel paced back and forth from the kitchen to the living room and Jessica locked herself in the bathroom. My thoughts turned back to God. I was irritated that I needed Him, because my anger towards Him was still raw. I closed my eyes and prayed, "God, I don't know why things like this happen when you have the power to intervene and stop them. Why didn't you blow a fierce wind and alter the course of the bullet? I don't know what to do now. I am so angry, and I want to curse at you or better yet, ignore you, but I need your help. Help me, God. Help me. Don't be silent now."

    I looked down at my hands and examined them. I moved the palms to my face and gently cradled my cheeks. I think I was checking to make sure I was still alive, because death was so nearby. The bathroom door opened and Jessica collapsed onto the mattress that served as her bed in the walk in closet. Again, I pleaded with God for some help and I made my way over and lay down on the bed next to her. She reached to turn on the television and popped a video into the VCR. Jessica stared at the screen and I stared at her. I brushed her hair with my fingers and prayed that God would have a loving and protective hand on her for the rest of her life. I closed my eyes and listened to the sound of her breathing, calm and rhythmic. Tears formed in my eyes and I fought desperately to keep them from coming, though I don't know why I couldn't just let them be. In my mind, I pictured my own brother and tried to imagine what it would be like if he had been torn from my life. The thought of it was too much to bear and the tears began to flow freely.

    Sometime around 3 o'clock in the morning, I made my way back to my own bed. I crawled under the covers, reached down to pick up my Bible, and turned to the Psalms. My eyes caught the words to Psalm 88 and I read them out loud to myself.

Psalm 88: 9-14

My eyes are dim with grief.
I call to you, O Lord, every day;
I spread out my hands to you.
Do you show your wonders to the dead?
Do those who are dead rise up and praise you?
Is your love declared in the grave,
your faithfulness in destruction?
Are your wonders known in the place of darkness,
or your righteous deeds in the land of oblivion?
But I cry to you for help, O Lord;
in the morning my prayer comes before you.
Why, O Lord, do you reject me
and hide your face from me?

I moved in and out of prayer and sleep until the first rays of sunlight hit my face. Groggy and wasted, I had trouble opening my eyes completely. Burning and swollen from crying, they pulsed like a heartbeat. My Bible was resting on my chest, still open to Psalm 88. I flipped the pages until I arrived at the book of Hebrews. I thought about the journey that lay ahead, anticipating that the life I had grown accustomed to would be vastly different now. My fingers worked their way to chapter 11, knowing that all hope for getting through this trial would be found there.

Hebrews 11:1-2

Now faith is being sure of what we hope for
and certain of what we do not see.
This is what the ancients were commended for.

I needed to have faith in God during a time when I could not understand or see Him. I decided to trust, despite my anger and the bitter feel of abandonment. In my heart I knew that there was nothing else to stand on; no other hope than the one offered to me by God. When nothing made sense, I chose faith in God's word.

I went to work that morning and carried on as I always did. It seemed so strange that the world kept working as usual. I felt like everything should be put on hold. Schools and businesses should close and everyone should stop what they were doing and be still to reflect and pray. But school was open and nobody I worked with knew that a child had stopped breathing the night before.

During my lunch hour, I went home to get something to eat because it hadn't occurred to me to pack my lunch. On my way back to school, I decided to drive by the place where Alberto had been killed. For some reason, I was drawn to that space. As I approached, a wave of nausea hit me and I opened the car door just in time to vomit in the middle of the street. I drove back home and called in sick. The reality of Alberto's death and the sadness I felt for the loss of him had hit me. I began to grieve for how much I would miss his baldhead, chunky cheeks, and sense of humor. Never again was I going to be able to hug him and pet the stubble on his head. As he got older, he wouldn't let me squeeze him as much, especially in front of his friends. I was like one of those old ladies with purple hair and knee high stockings that try and love on kids and send them running for cover.

Alberto had so much potential and character. He was a mini Chris Farley, full of humor and the ability to entertain. A man from church had even signed him up to take improve classes. I loved that kid and the idea that he was gone made me physically sick.

I also grieved for Jessica. She had already experienced deep pain in her life and I didn't know how she would be able to handle this. I worried about whether she and Isabel were going to be able to move forward with their lives. Jessica had planned on joining the Army, which I thought would be a wonderful way for her to become independent and see the world. She was scheduled to leave in October and I was afraid that she would spend the rest of her life in that little apartment on Gower Street, caring for her mom.

The week after Alberto's death, I was initiated into the world of gang life. Isabel and Jessica were receiving numerous phone calls daily, warning that Jessica was going to be the next target. The police tapped the phones and Jessica was forced to remain indoors. One night while we were over at Jessica's, Carrie leaned over to me and told me to move because I was too close to the window and would get shot if there was a drive by. Later that evening, Carrie told me that she always had a plan mapped out for which way she would dive for cover depending on where she was sitting. I never felt worried for my own safety, but I worried about Jessica and the other kids in the neighborhood.

Jessica began to get stir crazy sitting inside all day, so at night we would drive up to her building, and she would run out with her head covered by a sweatshirt and jump into the car. We drove around Hollywood, and into West L.A., where the reality of our lives seemed impossible amidst the trendy shops and houses with room for three cars in the garage. Jessica didn't have any desire to talk about how she was feeling and what she was going through. The music on the radio filled the silence and we all stared out the window, focusing intently on the images outside. Words, I found, were much more difficult to come by than they had been only a week ago. I tried to think of things to say to break the silence among us, but nothing sounded quite right. All of my thought were awkward and strange, unfit even for the ears of loved ones.

Several members of TMC stopped by to visit with Isabel during the evenings. It was hard for me to be civil to them because I placed a lot of the blame for Alberto's death on their shoulders. One night, about four days after Alberto had been killed, a group of us, including the gang members, Carrie and I, and some of Alberto's junior high friends, had congregated to talk about the funeral. Isabel wanted everyone's opinion about what Alberto should wear, as it was going to be an open casket. Isabel was worried about how he would look because the coroner had cut open his scalp during the autopsy. A fourteen-year-old girl reminded people of another friend of theirs who had been shot in the head. The family had put a beanie on him to cover it up. All of the youth chimed in with approval, affirming that the beanie had looked good on the dead boy. I sat in silence at a loss for fashion advice, in awe that this seemed to be a normal topic for these young kids. I was saddened at what their childhoods had become and the evil they had already experienced in the world. My mind wandered back to the concerns I had when I was fourteen. Life was all so fun and simple. The comparison brought on a sense of guilt at the drastic differences between my safe and secure upbringing and the violence that robbed the children in front of me of their innocence.

As I look back on the evenings spent surrounded by gang members with the constant threat of violence, I am struck by the fact that I never felt afraid that something might happen to me. The reasons are clear to me now, but back then they were hidden deep in my subconscious. I thought that my white skin was like a shield that would keep me safe. It never occurred to me that in the midst of another shooting, I might be hit; even by accident. White girls don't get shot in gang fights or drive by's.

Alberto died on a Sunday and was not buried until Saturday. We had a carwash in the church parking lot in order to help Isabel pay for the burial expenses. The memorial service was to be held at the Hollywood Forever cemetery. I was worried that something bad might happen and feared for the safety of Jessica as well as the other youth that would be attending the service. The week had been filled with the threat of violence and so far, nobody else had been hurt. The police had warned us that the potential for gang activity was heightened on the day of the funeral.

I arrived at the cemetery to learn that two of our high school boys had been shot the night before. They were standing in front of a popular nightclub on the corner of Melrose and El Centro when a car drove by and started firing at them. Ernesto was hit once in the leg and Justin was shot four times in the backside. They were both okay, but Justin was still in the hospital. Ernesto showed up at the funeral on crutches and acted like it was no big deal. He recounted the story to us in a dramatic fashion. As soon as they heard the shots, all of them ran into the club. Ernesto felt a sting in the back of his leg and looked down to see his pants filling up with blood. As soon as it was apparent that Justin was going to be fine, they roared with laughter that he had been shot in the ass. Toby was in the bathroom when the shooting started and heard the gunshots while he was on the toilet. He proudly announced that he hadn't been shot because he was taking a dump.

The TMC gang members arrived at the funeral wearing matching black t-shirts that said, "RIP El malo." Isabel was wearing one too. The gang members marched around the small church like they had been Alberto's best friends. I looked over at the youth who had been a part of the community house and had known Alberto for years. They were huddled in the back of the church, fighting to keep their emotions inside. Those kids were the ones that had spent a week each summer at camp with Alberto. They were the ones who had encouraged him and cheered for him at volleyball games. They were the ones that looked after him as if he were their little brother and sought to protect him from harm. My stomach turned inside me as I watched them wince in pain. All of them had battled for years to stay out of gangs and be involved in positive alternatives. The very gang members that were present at the funeral had beaten some of them in order to jump them into the gang. But despite the overwhelming pressures, those boys had protected each other and looked for other ways to be a part of something bigger than themselves.

At the end of the service, we lined up to walk over to the casket and pay our last respects. I was dreading this part of the service. I am not big on dead bodies, especially ones that have been dead for a week. When I die, I want people to remember me the way I was.

We all lined up in the packed little church to take our turn to say goodbye. I watched as people posed for pictures next to Alberto, sticking their face right down in the casket. Some people kissed him and shook his hand. Isabel was by his side the whole time, intermittently posing for pictures and crying out in grief. I looked around the room and noticed that all of the white people were petrified, while the Latino people looked like it was business as usual. It wasn't until months later that I took the time to reflect on the funeral and the lesson on cultural diversity.

My palms began to sweat as I moved closer to the body. I could see from a distance that Alberto was kind of a purplish color. He had on a beanie and looked peaceful with his hands resting at his side. The line moved slowly, as people took their time to examine Alberto's face for the last time. Finally, I found myself peering down at a boy who looked only slightly familiar. His facial features looked different, but there was definitely a peace in the way that his eyes were closed and his mouth was gently shut. I looked at his face and kept telling myself that it was Alberto lying in front of me. It looked to me like someone had made a wax replica of him, almost capturing his likeness to a tee. Isabel found someone with a camera to take my picture. I tried to act as naturally as possible, unsure whether to fake a smile or look sullen.

I remained at the front of the church while Alberto's friends circled around him. My love for them felt like a wet blanket that was smothering me. I felt overwhelmed by how much I cared for these youth and my desire to wrap them up in my blanket and keep them with me, away from the dangerous world. Some of them cried and some just stared at the body in front of them. My heart broke into a million pieces that day as we all realized the finality of it.

The people who worked at the cemetery came forward with the lid to the coffin. Isabel screamed and had to be held back as the top was sealed and Alberto's body was covered. Gang members in black shirts like marching ants swarmed forward to carry the casket out of the church. We moved aside as they grabbed a hold of the coffin and lifted it from its resting place. The ants moved swiftly through the aisle of the church, carrying their dead. Isabel was holding onto the casket, sobbing and trying to keep them from taking away her son.

The black shirts placed the casket in the hearse and the processional to the burial site began. A small group of us decided not to go to the cemetery where the burial was going to take place. We went to Dairy Queen instead. Looking back, it seems an odd thing to do, but at the time, comfort food seemed like the best option.

Isabel and Jessica had experienced an overwhelming amount of trauma, and it felt like they just kept getting more problems thrown in their direction. Alberto's father and Isabel's ex-husband, David, made the trip from Wyoming where he had been living the last ten years. He hadn't been a loving or present father while Alberto was alive, but he burst onto the scene expecting every one to cater to his poor, afflicted soul. David carved out a space for himself in Isabel's small apartment and demanded the attention of anyone who called around to visit and pay respects. He acted like somebody had jacked his car, as if Alberto was a possession of his that had been stolen. David was itching to put up a fight and knock somebody's teeth out of their head. The drinking didn't help matters. David had no shame and ruthlessly blamed Isabel for the death of their son. He told her that she should have done a better job watching out for Alberto and his death was a result of her negligence. This was coming from a man who had abandoned them and shirked all responsibilities as a father.

One evening, David had been drinking heavily for the entire day. His volatile nature was exacerbated and I was really worried about what he was capable of doing. I tried to get Isabel to kick him out of the apartment, but she wouldn't do it. At about two o'clock in the morning, I was completely exhausted and wanted to go home, but I was afraid to leave Jessica and Isabel alone with the crazy man. I longed for the comfort of my bed and warm blankets to hide under. Once again, I asked Isabel to kick David out and she refused. Finally, I left out of irritation and exhaustion.

The next day, I found out that David had raped Isabel in front of Jessica, while I was fast asleep in my bed down the street. When Isabel told me, all of the weight of everything that had happened since Alberto's death, came crashing down on my shoulders and broke me. I practically ran out of the apartment and I knew that my limit had been reached. All I wanted to do was go back home and sleep for a few months until life had calmed down and there wasn't a crisis around every corner. As I dragged myself down the street toward my apartment, I ran into my friend Rob. I broke down and sobbed and Rob gently placed his arm around me and allowed me the freedom to cry. He told me what I so desperately needed to hear. It wasn't my fault that Isabel had been raped. It wasn't my fault that Alberto had joined a gang and was killed as a result. None of it was my fault and yet I was carrying around a weight of guilt that I could have, should have done something to stop it all from happening.

Rob walked me home and for the first time, I understood that I was merely a servant, doing my best to walk along side a grief stricken family. I was not the Savior. I was humbled and relieved to know that the role I had tried to take on had already been filled long ago.

During the next two years, I would constantly have to remind myself that the responsibility for Jessica and Isabel was not mine to bear. It would take being overwhelmed and completely burned out to open my eyes to the fact that I could not save them from their pain. Now I can see the ways in which my own twisted desire to be needed and feel important was fostering impossible expectations. In many ways, I loved that Isabel came to depend on me because I felt special. Nobody else needed me like that and it gave me a sense of worth, even though it was also destroying me.

During the year following Alberto's death, I longed for somebody to come along and take care of me. My community was very supportive, but I didn't want to burden my friends. Most of them were involved with other families in the neighborhood and were overwhelmed as well. I imagined what it would be like to have a husband; to come home to a warm meal and loving arms to hold me. Sometimes, God just didn't seem like enough. I couldn't feel Him physically, and I craved the comfort of human contact.

I am grateful that some wonderful memories were also born during that difficult period. Two months after Alberto was killed, Jessica was scheduled to join the Army. The night before her plane left, she and all of the other brave eighteen year olds from Los

Angeles were put up at a hotel near the airport. Isabel and I went to the hotel with her, along with about five of Alberto's long time childhood friends. We ordered pizza and celebrated the new turn Jessica's life was about to take.

While the kids were eating and playing around, Isabel and I lay on the queen sized bed and she told me stories about Alberto. For the first time, it was not sad, but wonderful. Isabel talked about the time Alberto dressed up as a girl for Halloween. He wore high heels, make up and a dress. One of his friends started chasing him and trying to steal his candy. Isabel laughed at the memory of her son running down the street in women's pumps. It felt so good to laugh, because we had cried so much together.

When I returned home later that evening, I began to realize the ways in which I was being transformed. I felt different. Sadness had come into my life so suddenly and with so much force that I had forgotten what it was like to feel happiness. The intersection of joy in the midst of such deep sorrow was a gift that I don't remember ever having experienced. It opened my eyes to a new way of living. Joy is a blessing in normal circumstances, but when it comes during painful trials, it is like a whole new realm of hope that has unfolded.

I had known pain previously in my life, but through death, I have experienced sorrow on a new level. Nicolas Wolsterstorff wrote a book called, *Lament For a Son*, about the death of his son at the age of 25. I resonate with Wolsterstorff when he says that he shall look at the world through tears. Despite the deep pain, he acknowledges that he may see things that dry-eyed he could not. I have come to experience joy in the every day, ordinary things of life that never before caught my attention. Through death, I have experienced what it means to live. I have felt emotions that I didn't know existed. My heart knows new depths of pain but has a greater capacity to love and embrace simple pleasures.

The Dangerous Blonde

    Isabel was a short, stocky woman. She stood about 5'1, with broad shoulders and had strong, manly hands. Isabel's natural hair color was dark brown, but she had bleached her hair blonde for as long as I had known her. The style of clothing she wore was more suited for a teenager than for a middle aged woman. Baggy pants and vans tennis shoes were her uniform. From a distance, Isabel looked about sixteen, but she wore her age on her face.
    There was almost always music playing in the apartment, and Isabel had an odd collection of tapes. She enjoyed rap music, which was also Jessica's preference. But Isabel also had a tape of little kids singing to Jesus that she listened to all the time and it kind of freaked me out. The music actually sounded like grown-ups pretending to be little kids because it was so over the top. As soon as the tape ended and the last child had cried, "Senor, te amo (God, I love you)," the next voice was a rapper talking about gin and juice, bitches and ho's.
    One Thursday evening, I went over to Isabel's apartment with Carla and Melissa. The girls' were going to pick up Jessica to go and

see a movie with some friends from school, and I was on my way to help Isabel bleach her hair. When I arrived, Jessica was in the shower, running late as usual. Isabel had set up a mini beauty parlor in the living room. She handed me the hair dye kit and I began to pour and mix the ingredients. The smell was intense, causing all of us in the apartment to become a little bit loopy. I put on the plastic gloves that came in the kit and began covering Isabel's head with the blonde poison. She told me over and over to make sure I didn't miss any spots. I assured her that I was a professional, as I had been dying my own hair for over seven years.

When Jessica emerged from the shower, she pointed and laughed at her mother, whose hair was sticking up and out every which way. Isabel got up and went to the mirror to examine the crazy mop on her head. Upon seeing herself, she darted to the bathroom and shut the door. A minute later, Isabel emerged wearing bright red lipstick and dark eyeliner. She pranced around the apartment proclaiming, "Yo soy la rubia peligrosa (I am the dangerous blonde)." Then, she ran over to the closet and pulled out a pair of dusty high heels. Isabel put them on and went over to Jessica and began doing a dance in front of her. Carla and Melissa laughed hysterically, but Jessica hid her face in the pillows of the couch, embarrassed by her mother's antics.

The day after I dyed Isabel's hair, I was inspired to do my own. I wanted something cool and edgy, and decided to do streaks of white-blonde and black, alternating strips of my hair in the two colors. After waiting for thirty minutes, I rinsed my head and watched as the black water hit the tub and was sucked down the drain. As soon as I caught a glimpse of my wet hair in the mirror, I knew something wasn't quite right. I pulled out the hair drier and began to uncover the freak of nature that I had become. Apparently, the blonde and black had mixed and turned my hair blue. My first thought was that white and black should make gray, but smurf blue was sprouting from my head. The look I was going for was punk rock, not Marge Simpson. Leaving the apartment was no longer an option. I would have to call Christine and ask her to bring me some food and news of the world outside. Instead, I picked up the phone and called Isabel. Before I could explain my serious problem, she started going on about her own hair issues. Apparently, I had missed a spot, right in front. A patch of brown was nothing compared to the troll hair that was growing on my head. Isabel said she would be right over, and I knew it was as much out of a desire to ridicule me than it was to offer assistance. Isabel did not spare me any dignity and laughed in my face as I opened the door to let her in. I guess hair dying was not my forte after all, because right in front of her forehead, a little to the left, was a mound of brunette surrounded by a sea of platinum. We pointed and gawked at each other, attempts at beauty gone awry.

I through my hair into a ponytail and we headed down the street to Sav On to purchase some more dye. As I made my way toward the aisle with the hair color, Isabel grabbed my arm and pulled me toward the Pharmacy. Eager to get out of there as quickly as possible, I reluctantly followed her to the back of the store. Apparently, we needed to check our blood pressure. Isabel led me to the seat that had a machine attached to the armrest, and I sank into the chair, putting my arm through the hole. The machine cost a quarter, and Isabel shoved a coin into the slot. The plastic began to enlarge and tighten around my upper arm. Startled, I sat upright and winced as the pressure intensified. An old lady was sitting nearby, waiting for her prescription to be filled. She stared at us with a glare, as if we were children misbehaving. After it was determined that my blood pressure was normal, we went to find the hair dye. Isabel and I stood in front of the myriad of colors and brands, overwhelmed by the choices. Finally, I chose a deep maroon color.

Isabel applied the chemicals to my hair, and I told her to make sure that she didn't miss any spots.

A Birthday Celebration

In the Latino culture, a child's fifteenth birthday is a milestone that is greatly anticipated and elaborately celebrated. Families save their pennies in order to throw a party as costly and extravagant as a wedding reception. Alberto would have turned fifteen the April after his death. Eight months had passed and his absence was still sorely felt. Isabel had adorned her apartment with pictures of Alberto around every corner, one of which was nearly life size. His old t-shirts were hanging from doorways and curtain rods.

I saw Isabel or spoke with her on the phone nearly every day. Our lives were entwined in a strange net of dependence and obligation. I had promised Jessica when she left for the army that I would take care of her mother. I wanted Jessica to get out of the neighborhood and see that the world extends beyond the confines of Hollywood. The weight of that promise was intense and nearly impossible to fulfill. I was stupid to have believed that I possessed the strength and ability to live up to such expectations.

This was an opportunity to feed my struggle to feel needed and important. Part of my desire to help was out of a genuine motivation of love for Isabel and part of it was out of pride. If someone relied on me, then I felt valuable.

In many ways, I let go of much of my own life when I made that promise. Isabel's needs were so intense and constant. She was suicidal much of the time and often called me in the middle of the night needing company. I would arrive at her apartment, groggy and tired, to find Isabel cleaning because she thought that Alberto would be coming home.

Gang members were still coming around and bothering her. Sometimes, Isabel would call me to come over because several of the guys were convinced that I was an undercover cop. As soon as I showed up, they suddenly had some place else that they needed to be. Isabel started calling me "detective."

I arrived at the apartment one afternoon to find a young man named Jaime who was no more than sixteen years old sitting on her couch. I had never seen him before, but he proudly announced that he had been a member of T.M.C. for several years. It seemed hard to believe because he looked like a baby to me. I don't know why, but I began asking him questions about himself and his affiliation with the gang. Jaime had joined the gang when he was thirteen years old. I asked if it had been his choice or if he had been jumped in. Jaime acted like that was a crazy question. Of course he wanted to be in the gang. I continued my interrogation and asked him why. The answer was simple and not far from what most of us long for. Jaime wanted a place to belong. After acknowledging this, he began twitching and looked uncomfortable. Jaime had probably allowed himself to be more vulnerable than he was used to, which caused regret to crawl up and down his skin. I realized that my title of detective had been fed, and Jaime practically bolted out of his seat and out the door, surely on his way to tell the rest of the gang that their premonitions about me had been correct.

Even though Alberto was gone, Isabel could not stop living her life around him. She decided to plan a fifteenth birthday party for Alberto. I tried to be the voice of reason, but she insisted that we have a party at the cemetery. Isabel and I visited every florist on Santa Monica Boulevard to find the best price for flowers. As we looked through books of flower arrangements, she would always turn to the wedding section and pick out flowers for my wedding day. Then she would make conversation with every male we ran across in the hopes of making a match. Never mind that most of them were about fifty and stood five foot three. Isabel would point and nod without discretion at any man who was not accompanied by a female, whether he was standing on the street corner or in the grocery line.

Isabel finally decided on a nice arrangement of blue and white carnations for the party. We made phone calls and invited people from HUP and neighborhood friends. On April 17th, 2002, we picked up the flower arrangement and a cake and headed down to the cemetery. Three older gang members were already there when we arrived. I was unaware that they had been invited and was surprised to see them. I immediately felt protective and watchful over the kids who were on their way in the church van.

The rest of our group arrived and we all gathered around the two-foot by six-foot plot of grass that marked Alberto's grave. Isabel and I set the stand of flowers at the foot of the grave and we sang happy birthday. As we were singing, Dan, Amy and I were looking back and forth at each other with bewildered faces. Isabel got out the camera and we all posed around the flowers and then next to the grave marker. One of the gang members began to pour his beer on top of the grave and the others followed. They repeated, "Happy birthday, little homie." This seemed like a good time to cut the cake. We stood around the grave nibbling on chocolate cake and looking at each other awkwardly. Nobody spoke much. The adults were trying to figure out how to make this situation more comfortable for the youth and the youth were in quiet contemplation over the absence of their friend at his own party.

Darkness began to descend and mercifully announce the end of the festivities. Everybody hugged and said goodbyes except for the gang members who were still taking a sip of beer and then pouring one on the grave. Happy fifteenth birthday, Alberto.

The next milestone marked the year anniversary of Alberto's death. As the day approached, I began to reflect on the way that my life had gone from a relatively quiet existence, to a mode of constant crisis. I longed for the days of years past that seemed boring and uneventful.

I was grateful, however, that the end of this year was near and the possibility that it was time to move on. Isabel was still alive, which was a miracle. I often thought that we would bury her next to Alberto, where she longed to be. My hope was that the pain that pierced so deeply in that first year would begin to subside with the passage of time and every day would become more bearable. Isabel might now begin to believe that she could keep going and that there was a future for her even though Alberto was gone.

We began to plan for another ceremony. Isabel and I took a trip back to the florist to pick out yet another flower arrangement for the occasion as well as to get some more ideas for my bridal bouquet. Isabel needed that distraction and I went along with it, though I have no intention of carrying a collection of peach roses entwined with gobs of white and pink ribbon on the day I get married. The fact that I didn't even have a boyfriend was no reason not to be prepared for my big day. As we were flipping through the book of pictures, Isabel looked at me and said, "When you get a boyfriend, I want to meet him so that I can tell him to take care of you because you are a treasure." I cannot tell you what that statement has meant to me over the years. She spoke to a place inside me that had longed to hear those words and feared that they might never be spoken. I have had so much doubt about my worth and whether or not anybody could ever love me. But Isabel thought that I was a treasure and she was so sure that somebody else would too. All the pain and exhaustion of the last year were suddenly worth every minute because I knew that Isabel loved me for having endured with her and that love engulfed me to the point where I felt an overwhelming sense of worth and purpose.

On August 5th, 2002, we gathered at the community house for a service honoring the one-year anniversary of Alberto's death. Jessica was given a leave of absence from the Army and came home for the week. She stood by her mother during the service and I watched them from the back of the crowd. It was time for me to step back and let the two of them have this experience without me. Jessica had matured and looked healthy and strong. She kept one arm around her mother who cried and cried, and the other arm was wrapped across her chest as if she were embracing herself.

I don't remember much of what happened in the service. Now, I see the ways in which the anniversary marked a desire for me to close that chapter of my life. I was half way finished with my degree at Fuller Theological Seminary and I wanted to be able to put more energy and time into school and friendships. In other words, I wanted my life back. I loved Isabel and Jessica, but it was time for all of us to go on with our lives and look forward.

What happened the next day affirmed my thoughts and gave me the push I needed to begin to focus on the things in my life that had been put on the back burner. Isabel, Jessica and I had planned for the three of us to go to the cemetery to have a quiet ceremony of our own. Jessica drove, Isabel sat in the front seat with her cooler of beer and I sat in the back with the flower arrangement draped over me. Before entering the freeway, we stopped at a liquor store. Isabel handed Jessica and me some food stamps so that we could buy candy and soda. I had never used food stamps before and I felt guilty, but Isabel refused to let me use my own money. It was a strange feeling to hand the stamps to the cashier and walk away with my Dr. Pepper and a snickers bar. It almost felt like I had put them in my purse when no one was looking and made a quiet escape out the side door without paying. Once we had our snacks, we entered the freeway and fought the traffic. The windows were rolled down and the wind attacked me once we began to speed up. Jessica and Isabel were talking in the front seat, but I could not hear a word. As we exited the freeway in Glendora, I wiped my wind soaked face and removed pieces of hair that had stuck to my cheeks.

We drove through the maze of manicured grass and marble statues to the back of the cemetery. Jessica and I sat cross-legged next to the grave while Isabel lay down beside it with her head resting on the grave marker. She talked to Alberto as if he were still alive, telling him about his friends and how much she loved him. She spoke to him sweetly, like a new mother to her infant baby.

Isabel was drinking her beer and talking to her child in the hot August sun and as the hours passed, my ability to be a part of her grieving process were coming to an end. I got up to go for a walk to think things through and talk to God. As I walked along, I noticed the grave markers beneath me and the names and dates of life and death for children who never reached their fifth birthday. I felt like I should cry, but I had become numb to any feelings other than self pity for the situation in which I found myself. My compassion for others had run out and I was completely focused on my own inward battle. I felt sick at my lack of consideration for these lives cut short. I still had life and yet I was spending these precious moments feeling sorry for myself. But I knew that God accepted me the way I was and that pretending to be something that I am not is a big waste of my time. I told God that I couldn't continue to live my life around Alberto's death. I didn't even ask for Him to give me strength so that I could be a support to Isabel. I just told Him the way it was going to be. Usually, that blows up right in my face because God knows better than I do what I really need. But this time, I could feel Him looking at me and shaking His head the way a teacher would to a naïve student. I was trying to take the place of His Son and be the Savior, yet again. I really needed to stop doing that. When did I become so narcissistic as to think that my actions could keep Isabel alive or Jessica from feeling the pain of the loss of her brother? I had become so frustrated that my life revolved around Isabel, but I was the one who allowed it to happen and even sought it out because I wanted to be needed.

After thanking God for relieving me of my burden once again, I rejoined Isabel and Jessica. Kneeling down beside the grave, I felt the prick of the blades of grass on my knees and the warmth of the mud beneath them. I closed my eyes and spoke to Alberto. I have often wondered if people in heaven can hear when we speak to them. I sometimes tell my grandfather things, never knowing if my thoughts reach him. I told Alberto how much I missed him and how sad I was that he was gone from us. But now it is time for me to gather all of the memories that I have of you and store them in my heart. I won't forget about them or what your life has meant to me, but I need to live in the present and stop trying to live in light of the past. And then I shared with Alberto one of my favorite memories of him.

We had gone to a church coffee house that was put on once a month and raised money for HUP. An improv group provided the entertainment for the evening and two actors were on stage performing. They asked for two volunteers to come up and perform this next act with them. Alberto's hand darted for the ceiling because he loved to be the center of attention. He was called up to the stage and grinned with pleasure as he stood under the lights to see that the faces in the audience were fixed on him. The actors explained to the volunteers that their job was to insert a word into the conversation between the two actors whenever they paused in silence. The actor would begin a sentence by saying something like, "I am really hungry. I could eat a…" and the volunteer would finish the sentence. The scene began and suddenly, the actors started to argue. The man looked over at the woman and said, "You are a…"

I stopped breathing in that second and my eyes were focused intently on Alberto. This guy was setting him up for disaster. I could see that Alberto was thinking hard about what to say, censoring the first words that were on his tongue. I was bracing myself for the church's reaction to hearing, "You are a bitch, whore, slut, etc." It seemed the silence lasted for minutes as Alberto fought to think of an appropriate way to finish the sentence. And then, he looked up from his shoes as proud as could be and said, "Mean lady. You are a mean lady." You could hear the gasp as the audience collectively let out the air they had been holding in. Laughter and applause filled the church and Alberto was a star.

On our way home from the cemetery, Isabel wanted to stop at the restaurant Siete Mares in East Los Angeles for dinner. I really just wanted to go home and start what felt like a new life, where I let Jesus be Jesus and me be me. But I was not about to go against the wishes of a woman who lost her son that very day one year ago. Isabel was pretty drunk by this time, so Jessica and I helped her into the booth. She insisted that we order the siete mares soup to share and then we could each order whatever we wanted. The waitress came over and took our order of a beer, the seven seas soup, and some tacos.

Isabel gave Jessica some money for the jukebox and told her what songs to choose. She swayed back and forth to the music and announced at the beginning of each new song that this one was her absolute favorite. Soon, the waitress came over with a bowl of soup that looked like one of those bathtubs for babies. There were all sorts of legs and tails and claws hanging over the edge, trying to make an escape. We would pull one out and try to figure out what kind of animal it was. Once we determined it to be a lobster, we would examine the thing to figure out how to eat it. Each crab and shrimp was analyzed before being consumed. It was like a game, and I was beginning to have fun. I started to think that this life wasn't so bad and that maybe I could continue to be a part of this family.

After a few more beers, the tone changed and it became all too clear that it was time for me to step out of the role I had taken in the family. Isabel became emotional and sad about the absence of her son at the dinner table. She was sitting next to Jessica in the booth, looking across the table at me. She said, "Alberto would have been sitting where Mandy is now. We always used to be three. Alberto is gone and we were only two, but now with Mandy we are three again." I felt the legs and claws that were now in my stomach beginning to climb to the surface. Something inside me snapped, and I wanted to run out of the restaurant never to see Isabel or Jessica again. I had my own family, a mom and a dad and a brother who was still alive. This was not my family and I was not going to be the token replacement for a missing member. I felt like a child and wanted to crawl into my own mother's lap, lay my head on her chest and feel her kissing my forehead. I longed to see my brother and hold onto him so that he would never be taken away from me.

The next weekend, I got in my car and drove to San Diego to be with my own flesh and blood. I longed to be in a place that was nurturing and familiar, where I could be a child and have someone look after me. I needed to be reminded that I already had a place where I belonged; where I would receive unconditional love without having to try and be someone spectacular. I could just be myself with all of my faults and insecurities and my family would love me just like that.

Juan

Christine and I spent three long, and eventful years in the apartment on Willoughby Avenue before my sanity and patience had taken leave. One day, on a quick walk to the other end of Willoughby to visit my friend Rob, I saw a house that had never before caught my attention. There were several men inside and they were all dressed in white from head to toe, with paint splatter to add some color, and big construction boots. They were taking a break from the day's work and were digging their hands into brown lunch bags. I stared shamelessly through the window of the enclosed porch where they were seeking refuge. After debating whether or not to bother them, my eyes caught sight of the fabulous paint job and wood floors. My feet headed up the steps of the porch.

As I entered, the men simultaneously pointed to the living room, before I could even ask where the owner might be found. I stepped over their sprawled legs and made my way inside. The house was beautiful, with built in bookshelves, decorative hanging lamps, and a lot of character. The owner was squatted down under the sink, and

I whispered a shy, "Hello." He peeked his head out and asked if he could help me. I told him that he and his crew had done a wonderful job fixing up the house and was just wondering if it would be for rent. At the sound of praise, he jumped up and began showing me every inch of the house, describing in detail all the work that had been done, pausing long enough for me to express awe.

At the end of the tour, I learned some sad news. The rent was much too costly. I wanted that house so much that the thought of robbing a bank actually crossed my mind. But all hope wasn't lost. There was a back house that had also been redone which was much more in my price range. Upon hearing this news, I straightened back up from a slouched, moping position and followed the man down the driveway.

The second house was even more spectacular than the first, with painted wood ceilings, a built in desk, a breakfast nook, and a cool windy staircase that led to the bedrooms. Right then and there I told the man that I would move in as soon as it was ready.

As I walked down the driveway and headed to Rob's, my mind was wild with visions of interior design. New homes had been established for pictures and furniture, and I came up with a list of items that needed to be purchased. One month later, I found a shopping cart on the street that I loaded with boxes, walking back and forth from my old apartment on Willoughby to my gorgeous new house on Willougby.

Christine and I both have birthdays in May, one week apart, and we decided to have a luau birthday bash in our new home. We planned the party for weeks, organizing food and decorations. I was bursting with anticipation and excitement.

The party was planned for a Saturday night, and I had been in San Diego the night before to celebrate my birthday with family. I drove back to Hollywood on Saturday afternoon, eager to begin setting up for the party. I pulled into the driveway and practically jumped out of the car before it was completely stopped. I started to make my way to the bedroom to find my Hawaiian skirt, when Christine appeared from the kitchen. Instead of being dressed for a party, she was in sweats and her hair was in a ponytail. I was about to pick her up and throw her into the shower when she said, "Come and sit down for a minute." That never means good news. We sat down in the living room and I waited for her to give me an explanation. Finally, she said, "Juan was shot and killed last night." My body went limp and I felt like I had been struck by a bullet myself. It had not even been two years since Alberto's death.

It took me a while to collect myself and my thoughts enough to ask Christine what happened. The night before, while I was asleep at my parent's house, our neighbors across the street were having their own party. A man ran by on foot and began shooting at the group of people who had gathered outside on the street. Apparently, the gunman was seeking revenge on a guy named Freddy, and had intended to shoot him. In addition to wounding Freddy, he fatally shot Juan, who happened to be at the wrong place at the wrong time. Christine heard the gunshots and ensuing commotion at 12:30 in the morning. When she awoke the next morning, she received a phone call from Nancy, with news that another one of our kids had been killed.

Juan was a soft spoken and gentle boy, well loved and respected by the youth in the neighborhood. He was seventeen years old and was scheduled to graduate from high school in a month. Juan had participated in the boys Bible study at HUP for several years and never caused any trouble. He was the type of youth that parents hope their children turn out to be.

Needless to say, there was not going to be a luau that evening. I sat on the couch for about an hour, in shock. Numb and unable to feel sadness, or frustration, or anger, I just stared off into the distance.

Once I was able to function, Christine and I put a sign on the door to inform people that the party had been cancelled. The idea of having to explain what happened to our guests as they arrived seemed too overwhelming. After locking the door behind us, we headed across the street to join others who had gathered around a memorial of candles and flowers. I was not acquainted with any of the people who had congregated, but we all looked at each other lovingly, joining together to give and receive comfort. I sat down on the sidewalk and picked up a carnation from a vase that had been placed near me. I gently rubbed my face with the petals, feeling the softness against my cheeks and forehead. Placing the flower to my nose, I breathed in and was irritated to find that it didn't have any fragrance at all. I picked off some petals and began to grind them into the ground, leaving streaks of red on the sidewalk. The stem was to be my next victim and I broke it in half, using it to poke the eyelets of my tennis shoes. Then, I dragged it on the ground, drawing an invisible circle around myself. When I had finished, I tossed the stem aside and it landed in the gutter. I grabbed the rest of the flower and began picking at the remaining petals, deciding what their fate would be. In the end, I had mercy and placed the flower back in the vase, though it stood much shorter and was quite a bit more mangled than the others.

I looked around and Christine was gone. It had become dark without any warning and I felt disoriented. Without a fixed destination in mind, I began to wander down the street. I hadn't gone very far before reaching the apartment where Juan had lived. Several of the boys from the volleyball team who had been friends with Juan were sitting on the steps of the building, drinking beer and smoking pot. My first inclination was to reprimand them for using drugs and alcohol. That inclination quickly passed as I remembered the grief that they were experiencing for a second time. I actually felt honored that they didn't try and hide from me. As I made my way up the steps, I wrestled with the fact that I wasn't disturbed by their actions. It made sense that these youth would seek to alter their senses, even though it was not the healthiest way to deal with the pain. But again, I found myself to be the white girl, entering territory that had only recently become mine. My whole perspective had changed, and I no longer saw the world the way I used to. Whatever innocence that had remained from my childhood had slipped away. I felt like I was made up of steel and glass. Sometimes, life would hit me and it would clink against the steal before falling to the ground. Other times, it would hit and the glass would shatter, breaking me into little pieces.

I joined the boys on the steps, completely ignoring the joint that was being passed around and the beers in their hands. At that point in time, they were of little consequence. I hugged Jeffrey and whispered how sorry I was. He hugged me briefly, and then pulled out of my embrace. He began to ask questions, and I wasn't sure if he was addressing me, his friends, or God. "Juan was the best one of us, and of all people, he was the last one who would deserve this. First Alberto and then Juan. Why does this keep happening? Why does it happen to the innocent? Who will be next?"

I didn't have any answers, though I longed to provide them, but same questions were looming in my own mind. We stood in silence and I placed my hand on Jeffrey's shoulder. He kept his eyes on the ground, gently shaking his head back and forth. I found myself in a place that I prayed I would never be again; standing beside a child who was mourning the loss of a friend.

Tony, another member of the HUP volleyball team and Juan's cousin, appeared from the back of the building. At fifteen years old, he was one of the younger kids. Tony gave Jeffrey a little punch on the shoulder and stopped at the stair just above the one I was standing on. Without saying a word, he reached out, put his arms around my waste and squatted down a little bit so that he could rest his head on my chest. I felt like I was holding a three year old. Tony began to sob, gasping for air as he struggled to catch his breath. He shook violently in my arms, and I had to steady my feet to make sure we didn't fall over. I held him as he cried, and my glass casing began to crack.

After Tony was able to hold himself up, he quietly sauntered to the back of the building from where he had come. Inside, I was completely torn about what to do next. Part of me wanted to stay and offer comfort, providing a listening ear if nothing else. But another part of me was done with death and mourning. I still felt heavy from the weight of Tony in my arms. Even though he was gone, it was pressing me down, pushing me into the ground. And it was then that I realized that I didn't have the ability to offer anymore. After saying my goodbyes, I took off down the street feeling like a failure and a coward. I wished that I could have been strong and steady, a firm foundation to stand on. But I was weak and wasted, barely able to hold myself up.

Several days after Juan had passed away, it was time for another carwash in the church parking lot. Whenever I used to see youth giving a carwash to raise money, it was always for new basketball uniforms or a cheerleading trip. Now, a carwash means that someone has died and there isn't enough money to bury them.

We all gathered at the church with buckets and hoses, rags and soap. As I saw that familiar sight of kids playing in the water and splashing each other, an image of Juan popped into my mind. At the carwash for Alberto, he was chasing Jeffrey with a wet rag, and trying to smack him with it. It was an eerie feeling to know that Juan had been in that very place, washing cars for a funeral, and now he was the one that would be buried.

The carwash and other donations helped make it possible to have a funeral for Juan. When I arrived at the memorial service, the little church was packed. Out of the corner of my eye, I saw Isabel at the front of the church. I quickly looked away, hoping she hadn't seen me.

At the end of the service, everyone processed by the open casket. This time, I did not stare in disbelief when people were taking pictures and kissing Juan's cheek. In fact, it felt like this was how it had always been, and I had never known anything different. As I made my way to the front, Isabel found me and grabbed my arm. She did not let go of me as we walked around the casket, or as we walked to the burial site, or as we watched the casket being lowered to the ground. Isabel kept both hands firmly around my wrist, leading me where she wanted me to go. I followed obediently, like a well-trained puppy.

Isabel had a strange way about her, and it almost seemed like she was enjoying herself. She wanted to be right up close to what was happening, and kept comparing everything to Alberto's funeral. Isabel had a running commentary that she whispered in my ear throughout the entire burial process. When the time came to shovel the first scoop of dirt and drop it onto the casket, Isabel stood up halfway and leaned forward to get a better view. At the sight of the earth covering her child, Juan's mother screamed, and Isabel's grip on my arm tightened. She felt that scream to the core of her being and Isabel was the only one present who could have comprehended its meaning.

Isabel still had me by the hand as we walked back to the neighborhood, but somehow, it didn't seem as restrictive as it had before. When we reached her apartment, Isabel set me free, releasing the grip she had, not only of my hand, but also over my life. The pain that Isabel heard in the cries of another grieving mother touched something in her that I never could have reached. Isabel had tried to get whatever it was that she had been searching for and needing from me, but it was not in my possession. The day of Juan's funeral, I finally realized that what she had been looking for was understanding. Though I had loved and cared for Alberto, his loss meant something much different for me than it had for Isabel. We both had hopes for his future, but I never held him as a baby. We both admired his sense of humor, but I wasn't there when he learned to talk. I had my family and friends, as well as an education and a multitude of resources. Isabel had her two children.

African American Spirituality

The spring quarter of my second year in seminary, March of 2003, was extremely hard on me academically and emotionally. I was taking a class called Biblical Hermeneutics that required an incredible amount of reading and papers. Hermeneutics is the study of Biblical passages within the context in which they were written. We dove in depth into Old Testament stories such as the rape of Tamar and the murder of Uriah. I have tended to gloss over the Old Testament because it can be difficult to understand in addition to the fact that God and His people did some things that make me uneasy. Biblical hermeneutics forced me to analyze and dissect these passages that I had avoided.

The further we got into the class, the more my faith began to cloud with doubt. I did not want to pray or read my Bible. This God that I had loved and been so devoted to became a stranger to me. The loving God who had become a man in order to save his people was full of wrath. I could not reconcile the God of the Old Testament and the God of the New Testament in my head or my heart.

Spiritual darkness filled my life. I did not know who I was if I was not a child of God; living in His presence and relating with Him. I had heard of people who had gone to seminary and lost their faith and I was on my way to becoming one of them. The thought that someday in the future I would long for God's presence and kneel before Him seemed an impossibility.

During this time, my friend Carrie came for a visit on a break from her studies at Oxford. She was studying to be an evangelist, of all things, and kept talking about the Lord this and the Lord that and praise God, hallelujah. Thankfully, I am able to be honest with Carrie and I didn't have to pretend that I was as enthusiastic about my faith as she was.

On Sunday morning, Carrie and I went to First Presbyterian Church of Hollywood, the church she had attended before moving away. The guest preacher was supposed to be some big shot in campus ministry. I had actually heard of him, and was just daring him to say something that would be meaningful to me. He preached a sermon about a passage from the book of Phillipians. I kept looking at my watch and made my grocery list on the back of the offering envelope.

How did I get to this place, where the most important thing in my life, the one thing I want to live and die for, had become a joke, a bore, insignificant? There are times when I think about what Jesus has done for me and I get so overwhelmed that I want to drop to my knees in awe and thanksgiving. But somehow, doubt and apathy had crept in and I could have cared less about Jesus.

Despite my growing lack of faith, I continued to put myself in positions where God was the focus. I went to church, but did not participate. When people prayed or sang and expressed worship, my heart was not moved and my head kept telling me that it was all bull shit. For some reason, I kept going every Sunday even though I had no intention of actively participating.

Prior to entering into this spiritual crisis, I had signed up for a two-week summer intensive class called "African American Spirituality." I was actually looking forward to this class because my hardened heart had just enough room in it for hope. Hope led me to a desk in the second row on that first day of class, when I usually opt for a seat in the farthest row to the back. I don't know how to explain it, but something began to change in me the minute I sat in that room and looked up to see the professor walk through the door. Kindness and love radiated through him before he even spoke a word. When he finally addressed the class, he introduced himself as Dr. J. Alfred Smith. I will never forget what he said after that.

"I sure hope you like me because I am going to love you."

I felt his love already and it reminded me of what it was like when I knew that God loved me. I sat in the second row and stared at this man, anxious to embrace him and soak up what he was going to teach. I wanted to possess the qualities that drew me to Dr. Smith and be a person of integrity and honor.

It is difficult to know where to begin to explain how profoundly African American Spirituality has affected me, because I was transformed in so many areas of my life by Dr. Smith, my classmates, and courageous African Americans throughout history. The class initiated a turning point in my life and brought healing where I didn't even know it was needed.

Dr. Smith fostered an environment of self-expression, and security. He led the way by sharing painful parts of his life, unafraid to cry in front of us. We were all able to become vulnerable with Dr. Smith and each other because of the atmosphere of support and encouragement.

The topic on our third day of class was the hip-hop movement and rap music. I have struggled a lot with this type of music and the messages it sends to the youth who listen to it. In one of the last pictures taken of Alberto before his death, he was wearing a t-shirt that said "C-Murder" across the front. C-Murder was a rap artist whose lyrics included shooting people in drive by's. The message he sent in his music seemed to perpetuate the atrocities he rapped about. It is hard not to correlate the music kids listen to with the violence that continues to occur in their lives.

One of my classmates brought two songs to share with the class along with a copy of the lyrics. Before playing the songs, she spoke to the class about the connection she feels to this music as an African American woman. The songs are a way for her to identify her own experience through the reflections of the artists. My walls went up before the first song even began and I was prepared to be offended and annoyed.

The songs that were played contained none of the cuss words, degradation of women, and violence that I hear in the songs that the youth I have worked with listen to. The two songs she played were actually beautiful and moving. I would not have a problem with the musical genre if the lyrics were along the same lines as the ones I heard in class, but the majority are not like that. I want to be sensitive to the fact that the artists are talking about the hard life they have experienced. It seems, however, that they are perpetuating this experience in their communities by talking about the drugs and violence in a way that glorifies them.

Sheepishly, I raised my hand though I had no idea what was going to come out of my mouth. I just knew that strong feelings had been elicited inside me and I needed to process them with the class. I looked down at my white skin and had second thoughts about speaking out. My mouth opened and my voice trembled as I began to speak. I offered up my concerns that most rap music is not like the songs that we had just heard. I want to be able to relate to the youth that I work with, but sometimes I don't know how because of vast difference in our backgrounds. As a white woman, it is difficult for me because this music has become such an integral part of these kids' identities, and I cannot relate to it. I feel sad that they want to listen to it and sadder still because it touches on their own experience of the way the world works. I wondered aloud how I could possibly make a difference in the lives of these youth. By this last sentence, tears had begun to roll down my face.

Dr. Smith looked down at his shoes and said, "My, my," while shaking his head back and forth. He lifted his head up and rested his eyes on me. Then, he asked me to stand up and come over next to him. I nervously arose from my seat and made my way to his side. He reached over and gently took my hand and held it in his. We must have been a sight to see, standing there in front of that class, an elderly black man standing about 5'5 holding hands with a young white girl towering over him at 5'11. Dr. Smith squeezed my hand in his as he looked up at me and said, "Your white skin is beautiful. Your blonde hair is beautiful. Your blue eyes are beautiful. The youth will see the genuineness of your heart and the love you have for them and that will mean more to them than your skin color or a shared history."

My classmates shouted, "Amen" and poured out support and approval. Dr. Smith let my hand go and I reluctantly removed it from his grasp. I wanted to hold his hand forever.

It was this experience that opened my eyes to a battle that had been raging within me for the last five years. I have hated my white skin. I want to look at my hands and see brown or black or purple. Any other color would do. Because I had embraced liberation theology and the idea that God loves the poor and oppressed, I didn't completely believe that He could love me too. I didn't know how God could be good if he weren't devoted to the people who had been outcast by the world. But what did that mean for me, a middle class white girl?

With this one small gesture, Dr. Smith answered the question that had been looming in the back of my mind. Yes, I am loved. Dr. Smith had told us never to write anyone off because of skin color or class. I had written myself off.

The crux of my struggle and confusion over skin color was the desire to be understood. The death of Alberto, dealing with gang members and issues of injustice seemed to separate me from my peers. I wanted to wear my pain and the pain of Isabel around my neck like a pendent so that people could look at me and know my story. But life doesn't work that way and those around us can only truly know us if we have the courage to let them into our world. The problem was, there wasn't a context for my reality among the carefully tended grass and serene skyline of Pasadena. I couldn't bring myself to share during the lunchtime conversations that I had spent the weekend picking out the perfect floral arrangement for the fifteenth birthday of my friends' dead son, while others shared about a funny movie they had seen or a new Italian restaurant that we just had to try. I felt isolated and alone, not knowing how to translate the things that happened at home to my life at school.

Because of this, I was drawn to the students of different ethnicities than my own. In a conversation that I had with an African American classmate, I learned that she has had to translate everything that we are taught in class in a way that would apply to her life. People who have grown up as minorities in the dominant white culture have been dealing with this all of their lives, whereas for me, it was new territory.

Now, I look at people and wonder about their lives; the things they are going through that can't be seen from the outside. The lady in the grocery line in front of me or the man who takes my ticket at the movies, the teenage goth walking down Sunset or members of my own family who put on a happy face to mask life's troubles.

All this makes me realize that there is beauty in revealing the struggles that rage inside. For me, the pain that is hidden stabs more fiercely than that which has allowed the light to touch dark corners and expose brokenness. A certain freedom arises from accepting ourselves enough to be real and open with others. Some people may not accept us, and we move past hurt feelings and damaged egos to find those people who will. Otherwise, we are doomed to isolation and loneliness even if friends surround us.

The doubt that was seeking to suffocate my faith faded as I came alongside a people who have known true suffering and yet have an abundant and joyful assurance in God. The African American community is well acquainted with oppression and grief, persecution and sadness, but through the years, it has been an unshaken faith in God that has given them hope. It was such a joy for me to worship with them, because they know how to praise and give thanks in the midst of sorrow. I needed to learn how to say, "Thank you, God. Despite all of the pain in the world, You are good and I am grateful for all of the blessings in my life."

Community

Community has become for me like air or food or water, a necessary element for survival. In a time when our culture values individuality and self sufficiency, I have been blessed with the opportunity to experience support and vulnerability with a group of people who were committed to being intentional about relationships and present with one another through joy and suffering.

A group of about twelve of us, who had been through the city dweller program and had stayed in Los Angeles after our year of service, began to meet once a month for community night. Most of us saw each other much more frequently, as we were friends and lived only blocks apart, but community night became a sacred time where we would gather for a potluck and fellowship. We called it, "the holy spirit potluck" because we each brought what the spirit led (or whatever we happened to have in the refrigerator). This meant that there were nights when we had lasagna, pasta salad, bread, and spaghetti, or a supper comprised of three different types of brownies.

After dinner we would share our prayer concerns, study a passage of scripture, do an art project, or play a game. We took turns planning the evening activity until somebody came up with the idea of sharing our life stories with one another. Each month, one person would bring pictures and share the memories, milestones, and challenges that have made each of us who we are today. We would gather around the brave person who let us have a glimpse into their history and pray for them. The process was very emotional and many of us wept as we discovered painful pasts and obstacles overcome by friends we had known for years. At the time, I had no idea how powerful it would be for me to know and be known in such an intimate way.

We spent over a year taking turns sharing our stories. Every time somebody bared his or her soul in all its beauty and brokenness, my heart was filled with an outpouring of love. I found that in telling my story and in hearing the stories of others, the revelation of those painful trials that are so often kept hidden even from those we are closest to, brings a level of healing and new life that I didn't know was possible. When Nancy, Stacey, Rob, Karen, Christine, Catherine, Alastair, Cindy, Pat, Carey, and Amy trusted me with intimate details of their lives, they placed a great deal of trust in my hands, hoping and believing that I would love them more deeply rather than judge them. We fear that if people know who we really are, with all of our faults and insecurities, that we will be rejected and unwanted. It is a courageous step to let others into those places and trust that we will be accepted and maybe even loved because of them. And this is the healing that I found in sharing all of me. Instead of scaring people away, I drew them closer to me as partners in my life's journey, a source of encouragement and accountability, of unconditional love and acceptance. The joy of being known in my weakness and doubt, and yet loved completely, is a blessing that I cherish. My community has been a precious gift for which I shall be eternally grateful.

Living in community can also be very challenging. Christine, Nancy, and I had become very close in our first few years of living in Los Angeles. We spent a lot of time together and poured out support and encouragement to one another. After Alberto's death, however, Nancy went through a difficult time in her life and needed Christine and me to be there for her more than ever. I was feeling very overwhelmed and drained from being by Isabel's side, and didn't have any energy left to support Nancy. I began to distance myself from her, unable to give anymore. This broke Nancy's heart, causing a rift in our friendship. We spent many months apart, only speaking occasionally. The depth that we once had was gone, and conversations became superficial. We were all hurting for one reason or another, but the bond of friendship that had seen us through painful trials in the past was in danger of breaking.

Nancy took the first step toward mending the friendship, and she had been the one most hurt by it. She called Christine and me one evening and suggested that we go to family therapy with Julie, a former city dweller and therapist. I had never been to family therapy with my own family, much less my friends. It seemed to me that friendship shouldn't be that much work, and I was exhausted and emotionally drained from Alberto's death.

Three weeks later, I sat on a couch in Julie's office, clinging to a pillow and refusing to make eye contact with anyone. The session was to be an hour and a half long, and after the first hour, the session had done more harm than good in my opinion. We were all honest about the disappointment, rejection, and frustration we felt for each other. What had been silently understood was now echoing back and forth between the walls of the tiny office. None of us was willing to admit fault and apologize. Each of us felt that we were right in feeling the way we did. We all looked desperately at Julie to take sides and put the others in their place. But what she did instead was far more helpful. Julie helped us to see and acknowledge the other person's point of view, without having to admit that any of us were wrong. It was okay for me to feel overwhelmed and unable to offer Nancy a shoulder to lean on, but I was able to see that this caused her pain and that she was entitled to feel the way she did. Nancy understood that I was in a difficult place, giving all of the energy that I had within me to Isabel, but asking me to save some for her as well.

We left Julie's office with a renewed sense of hope for our friendship. It may seem extreme to go to family therapy with friends, but Christine and Nancy were worth it. It took a lot of courage for Nancy to make it happen.

Even though we made great strides in renewing our friendship, it was not what it had once been. Nancy had been very hurt and was reluctant to trust me. My pride kept me thinking that I had been justified in not being there for her during such a difficult time in her life, and I had not apologized. We were friends again, but we often still walked on eggshells around each other.

Nancy had decided to move back to her hometown in Virginia to attend nursing school. She had a big going away party with our community, her friends from church, and her swim team. After playing Nancy's favorite games and eating a delicious meal, we congregated in the living room of our host. We each had an opportunity to share a story about Nancy or a blessing to send her on her journey. I sat on the floor and hugged me knees to my chest, listening to people voice their love and appreciation for Nancy's sense of humor, vulnerability, and loyal friendship. I knew that every word they said was true, and watched as Nancy tearfully accepted each blessing. Originally, I had planned to share a funny story, maybe from the trip we took to Hawaii, or the time she made us walk two miles home from a club at three o'clock in the morning. But as I heard everyone share, it occurred to me that Nancy had meant more to me than the goodbye story I was going to offer.

As soon as my mouth opened to say my piece, a lump formed in my throat, making it difficult to speak. I had to stop and compose myself as the person sitting next to me handed me a tissue. I tried again to form the first sentence, and my voice dropped into a weepy squeak. I realized that I was not going to get through my speech without crying, and my community encouraged me that it was okay to keep going. I told Nancy that she had been by my side during my most difficult time, the darkness of my depression, and when the tables were turned and she was the one in need, I was not there for her. It took me two years, but I was finally able to admit that I had failed her. I apologized for not having been a better friend, for being a source of pain in her life and for being selfish. I had been holding tightly to my pride, justifying the awful way I had treated a dear friend. Nancy came over and hugged me, again comforting me in my time of need.

At the end of the night, members of my community came up and hugged me, telling me how proud of me they were. I was reminded again of the beauty of having my weakness displayed for everyone to see, and being loved all the more for it.

Nancy called me the next day to accept my apology and thank me for making it. It is amazing how hard it is to admit fault when the hope of reconciliation and forgiveness are what lie right around the corner.

Nancy packed up all her belongings and sent them across country in a moving van. A few days later, she followed in her car. I received phone calls from Nancy every day for the next few weeks, as she craved the community and relationships she had just left behind. Nancy lasted all of six weeks in Virginia before she got right back in her car and headed toward L.A.

I moved back home to San Diego a few weeks before Nancy moved to Virginia. I had finished my degree at Fuller and was unsure of what to do with my life. Unfortunately, contemplating my future did not pay the bills, and I could no longer afford my rent.

I had my own goodbye party, given by the community. We spent the evening telling stories about all of the things we had been through together. Rob brought up the story about the two-mile walk home from the club. It is one of our favorites. After an evening of dancing at The Crush Bar, Nancy and I led the way down Cahuenga Boulevard as everyone else followed in bewilderment about twenty feet back. Rob kept shouting, "I am such a follower," because he had advocated for calling a taxi, but followed the masses down the street. At one point, I lay down on the sidewalk as Nancy and I waited for the others to catch up. She had invited a friend from work who turned out to be rather sleazy, and he kept trying to run off with Cindy. Rob came to her aid several times on the dance floor and the walk home, practically peeling the guy off her leg. It was important for me to remember all of the funny and wonderful events of the last five years, because sometimes it felt like pain and sorrow were all I knew of Hollywood.

    I saw the opportunity to leave Los Angeles as a relief. I was running away, trying to escape the brokenness and death. I had not recovered from the deaths of Alberto and Juan. They haunted me, filling my head with images of grieving mothers and children. I wanted to go away to a place where I would not be reminded of them; to the suburbs where I could smell my mothers stew cooking in the kitchen, hear the wheels of my dad's car pulling into the driveway as he came home from work, and stare at the lemon tree in the back yard, with little that resembled a place with so much pain.

    But as I spent the next few months in San Diego, I realized that Los Angeles was my true home. I desperately missed my friends, longing for the days when I could walk a few steps and be at their front door. The beauty and joy of relationships and the neighborhood came back to me, and the memories that filled my head were from happy times, playing with kids and laughing with friends. After spending five months in San Diego, I got a job as a bilingual coordinator at an elementary school in Hollywood.

Rekindled Hope

Today is January 1, 2005, and I am writing the last edition to this memoir. I spent New Year's Eve with Nancy and Christine, just as it should be. We went out to dinner and Nancy told us all about the three different guys she is dating. Christine and I chimed in with advice between bites of barbeque chicken and pad thai noodles. Then, we spent the evening drinking champagne and watching the A&E special of Jane Austen's, *Pride and Prejudice*. I can't think of a better way to ring in the New Year than with Mr. Darcy, the main character in the movie, and my friends. The three of us would look at each other and sigh as Mr. Darcy stared longingly at Elizabeth, the woman he loved. He is the type of man to which all men should aspire.

Before going to sleep, we all piled on Nancy's bed and talked about our hopes for 2005. I am determined to be less cynical and bitter this year. I used to be a hopeless romantic, but love had become a foreign idea rather than a hopeful possibility. I recently read a poem called *Aimless Love*, by Billy Collins that captured me to a tee.

Collins fell in love with simple things, from the shadows of an autumn evening, to a wren he saw while walking along the lakeshore. In his poem, Collins notes:

> This is the best kind of love, I thought,
> without recompense, without gifts,
> or unkind words, without suspicion,
> or silence on the telephone.

Even still, he acknowledges that his heart is always propped up on a tripod, ready for the next arrow to hit.

That is how I have lived, falling in love with things that are safe. I have desperately been trying to protect myself from the slightest hint of rejection and heartbreak. Fear had taken over any inclination I once had to live passionately.

But now, I feel that I am ready to risk in all the different facets of my life. Someone like Mr. Darcy came along and reminded me of what it felt like to desire companionship and love. He is a gentle and kind man, whose humility suggest a depth of character that I long to uncover. The sight of him is perfect, and yet it is his gentle nature that attracts me to him. To me, he is wonderful.

I can remember the first time I began to understand about romantic love. I was a sophomore in high school and was assigned the book, *My Antonia*, by my English teacher. I can remember reading the words Jim spoke to Antonia, and feeling that an entirely new aspect of life had been revealed. He told her that he thought of her more often than anyone else in the world. Jim wished he could have been her brother, or father, or husband, longing for something that would bind them together. As they were parting for the last time, Jim fought the darkness to memorize Antonia's face, which he vowed always to carry with him.

I knew that I could love someone that deeply. It became my secret hope that maybe, someday, someone would feel such adoration for me.

As it turned out, my Mr. Darcy did not find me to be the woman he had been searching for, but I will go on living and hoping for love. All that I have been through has shown me that the pain of loss in all its forms does not write my future. C.S. Lewis wrote in his book, *A Grief Observed*, that sorrow is not a state, but rather a process. At one time, the pain was like a fire and I was sitting in the middle, swallowed whole by flames. But in the process of grief, my scorched body moved slowly out of the burning timber. New skin is forming where the dead layers had peeled off. Now, I sit near the fire at a safe distance. I can feel the warmth on my face, and when the wind blows in my direction, the heat stings and reminds me of old wounds. I am changed forever; there is no doubt about that. Sorrow is a part of me, it is in my character. But seeing it as a process has opened up new possibilities where joy and hope can enter in.

The struggle throughout my life has been to seek God and love Him, whether I am burning alive or basking in warmth. It has also been a struggle to learn to love myself. Now, I am able to see myself more closely to the way that God sees me. To Him, I am not this body. I am not white skin or tattoos, I am not thin or fat, and I am not my facial features. All of the things that have caused me to doubt myself and my worth are not of any consequence to God. And it is His opinion and His love that is more important than that of any person. I have always known this to be true, but it has been difficult to live in this freedom.

It has taken me a year, almost to the day to finish this book. I began to write my thoughts as a way to process the time I spent with HUP and other significant events in my life. It has also been a way for me to say thank you to all of the people whose stories are entwined with mine. I have come so far, from the depths of depression and grief to a state of contentment. It has been God's faithfulness and the love of my family, friends, and community that have made the difference. I am no longer ashamed and will not hide my innermost thoughts and struggles, for having been accepted and loved despite them has brought me great peace.

I feel like it is time for a new story to unfold, one that has not been told before, at least by me. I am expectant and hopeful, looking forward with joyful anticipation, for what will come next.

> Psalm 52:8-9
> But I am like an olive tree
> flourishing in the house of God;
> I trust in God's unfailing love
> forever and ever.
> I will praise you forever
> for what you have done;
> in your name I will hope,
> for your name is good.

References

Cather, Willa (1918). *My Antonia.* Boston: Houghton Mifflin Company.
Collins, Billy (2002). *Nine Horses.* New York: Random House.
Lewis, C.S. (1961). *A Grief Observed.* London: Bantam Books.
Nouwen, Henri (1981). *The Genesee Diary.* New York: Doubleday.
Stavesacre (1996). At The Moment. On *Friction* (CD) Seattle, WA: Tooth and Nail Records.
Wolsterstorff, Nicholas (1987). *Lament For a Son.* Grand Rapids, MI: William B. Eerdmans Publishing Company.

Printed in the United States
41806LVS00002B/442-543